the
ley

Peter Harbison

Treasures of the
Boyne Valley

Original photographs by Tom Kelly

GILL & MACMILLAN
in association with THE BOYNE VALLEY HONEY COMPANY

Personal Acknowledgements

A book of this size, with so many pictures, cannot see the light without the help of many friends and acquaintances, and I would like to take the opportunity here to thank them one and all for their assistance. For the provision of, and permission to use, certain illustrations I would like to thank most sincerely Tom and Valerie Kelly of Drumree; Norma Jessop, custodian of the Special Collections in the Library of University College, Dublin; Tony Roche of Dúchas, who goes out of his way to be helpful, as do Joanna Finegan and Avice-Claire McGovern of the Prints and Drawings Department of the National Library of Ireland; Michael Kenny, Raghnaill Ó Floinn and Niamh Deegan of the National Museum of Ireland; Professor David McConnell, Dr Bernard Meehan, Marcella Senior, Aisling Lockhart, Brendan Dempsey and the Board of Trinity College, Dublin; David Griffin, Simon Lincoln, Colum O'Riordan and Hugh Doran of the Irish Architectural Archive; David and Edmund Davison of Davison Associates; Marcia Kenna, Stuart Cole and Ciarán O'Boyle of James Adam Salerooms; Geraldine Kennedy and Caroline Walsh of *The Irish Times*; Siobhán O'Rafferty, Petra Schnabel, Karl Vogelsang and Patrick Kelly of the Royal Irish Academy; Andrew Bonar Law, whose Neptune Gallery is always a treasure house of old engravings; Jan de Fouw for his remarkable engraving of the Boyne salmon; Christine Casey and Yale University Press for the plan of Newtown Trim and, too late though heartfelt, Muriel Brandt (died 1981) for her present of the Bective watercolour. Deirdre Rennison Kunz has been very supportive in giving this book its final shape, and the work of Síofra Gavin in researching some pictures is also much appreciated.

Many others also deserving of thanks have helped in various ways: Professor Anne Crookshank, the Knight of Glin, Dr Edward McParland and David White for ascriptions and dating of watercolours; Mairéad Dunlevy for help with silver; Angela Lally, Bellinter, and Richard Robinson of Newbury Hall, for access to their premises; Letitia Pollard, Editor of *Ireland of the Welcomes* for help in sourcing pictures; Josephine Shields for having brought me to the grave of John Boyle O'Reilly; and Claire Tuffy and her splendid team at Brú na Bóinne for never-failing courtesy. Finally, my thanks to Malachy McCloskey, of Boyne Valley Foods, and Fergal Tobin of Gill & Macmillan, without whose vision this book would not have happened.

Peter Harbison
June 2003

Gill & Macmillan Ltd
Hume Avenue, Park West, Dublin 12
with associated companies throughout the world
www.gillmacmillan.ie

© Peter Harbison 2003
0 7171 3498 9

Design by Haldane Mason Ltd, London
Map (pages 6–7) by Cartographica Limited, Derby
Printed by Butler & Tanner Ltd, Frome

This book is typeset in Bulmer MT, 10 on 14 point and Walbaum, 8 on 14 point.

The paper used in this book comes from the wood pulp of managed forests.
For every tree felled, at least one tree is planted, thereby renewing natural resources.

A CIP catalogue record for this book is available from the British Library.

1 3 5 4 2

Contents

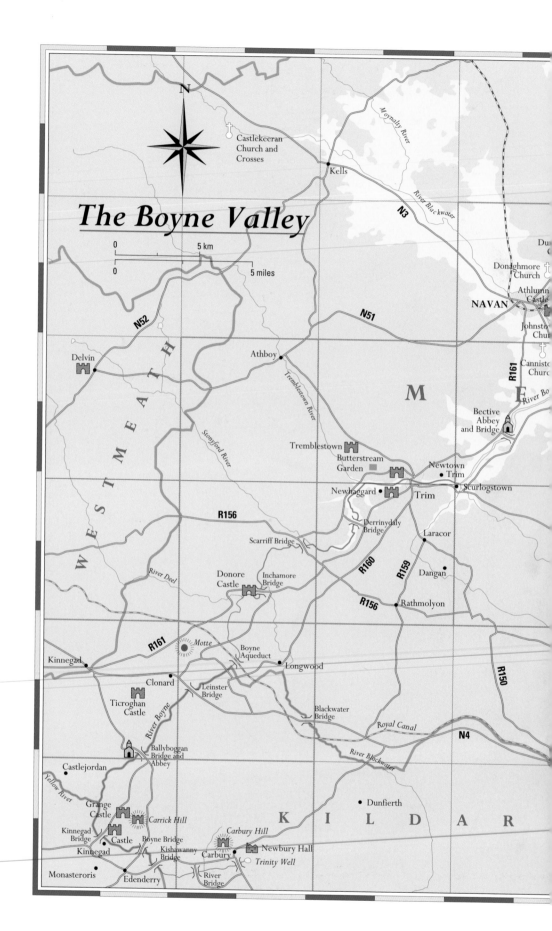

The Boyne Valley

Castlekeeran Church and Crosses

Kells

Moynalty River

River Blackwater

N3

N51

Du

Donaghmore Church

Athlumn Castle

NAVAN

Johnsto Chu

R161

Cannisto Churc

N52

Delvin

Athboy

Tremblestown River

River Bo

M

E

Bective Abbey and Bridge

Stonyford River

Tremblestown

Butterstream Garden

Newtown Trim

Newhaggard

Trim

Scurlogstown

R156

Derrinydaly Bridge

Laracor

W E S T M E A T H

River Deel

Scarriff Bridge

R160

R159

Dangan

Donore Castle

Inchamore Bridge

R156

Rathmolyon

R161

Motte

Boyne Aqueduct

Longwood

R150

Kinnegad

Clonard

Leinster Bridge

Ticroghan Castle

River Boyne

Blackwater Bridge

Royal Canal

N4

Ballyboggan Bridge and Abbey

River Blackwater

Castlejordan

Yellow River

Dunfierth

Grange Castle

Carrick Hill

K I L D A R

Kinnegad Bridge

Castle

Boyne Bridge

Carbury Hill

Kinnegad

Kishawanny Bridge

Carbury

Newbury Hall

Trinity Well

Monasteroris

Edenderry

River Bridge

0   5 km

0   5 miles

Monasterboice

Clogherhead

L O U T H

Mattock River

Mellifont
Abbey

King William's
Glen

Site of the
Battle of
the Boyne,
1690

Baltray

Townley Hall

DROGHEDA

Beaulieu

Monknewtown

Boyne
Navigation

Mell

*Inbher
Colptha*

Ledwidge
Cottage

N51

Mornington

dexter
tle

Slane

Oldbridge

*Dowth
Megalithic Tomb*

Colp

Irish Sea

Knowth
Megalithic Tomb

Brúgh na Bóinne
Interpretative Centre

Beauparc

Rossnaree

Laytown

oyne

*Newgrange
Megalithic Tomb*

chan
ch

N2

Duleek

River Nanny

M1

R150

Gormanston

Athcarne
White Cross

Annesbrook
Cross

Balrath Cross

*Fourknocks
Megalithic Tomb*

**T
H**

BALBRIGGAN

R108

N1

D U B L I N

N3

Dunshaughlin

R155

Ashbourne

N2

SWORDS

MALAHIDE

R108

N1

N3

D U B L I N

YNOOTH

N4

For further details consult the Ordnance Survey Discovery Series maps Nos. 42, 43 and 49

Introduction

By the cromlech sloping downward,
Where the Druid's victim bled,
By those towers pointing sunward,
Hieroglyphics none have read,
In their mystic symbols, seeking,
Of past creeds and rites o'erthrown,
If the truths they shrined are speaking
Yet in litanies of stone.

Perhaps it is appropriate that I should introduce this book with lines from the poetess Speranza, for they include references to ancient stone monuments in the Valley of the Boyne, itself named after the legendary goddess figure Bóann. Bóann's equally mythical husband Nechtan, or Nuada-Neacht, was the possessor of a secret well which was to give rise to the River Boyne, called Bovinda ('bright cow' or 'she who is bovine and bright') in Ptolemy's second-century map of Ireland.

Speranza (Lady Jane Wilde, 1826–1896) was the wife of Sir William Wilde (1815–1876), a polymath, folklorist, statistician, physician and many other things besides. Being also a man of no mean antiquarian interests, he

Arguably the most famous of Ireland's rivers, the gently-flowing Boyne was brilliantly described in flowery prose more than a century and a half ago by Sir William Wilde, whose journey downstream from the source to the sea is followed and brought up to date in the ensuing pages.

set about writing one of Ireland's most magical travel books, *The Beauties of the Boyne, and its Tributary, the Blackwater* (1849), published just over a century and a half ago, in which he quoted his wife's stanza cited above. The first and best of all the books about the Boyne, Wilde's work is illustrated by atmospheric woodcuts that complement his own inimitable style of writing and give us something of the flavour of the era in which he wrote. Text and illustrations were reproduced in slightly abbreviated form exactly a century after its first appearance by Colm O Lochlainn of the Three Candles Press, who described Wilde as 'the first and still the greatest of our scientific archaeologists'.

It is the wide interests of its remarkable author that make *The Boyne and the Blackwater* such a fascinating read, and one which preserves some long-lost local traditions which I will have reason to recall in the pages that follow. Like many another Victorian book, it has its share of purple prose, some of it too high-blown for modern taste. But one can, nevertheless, have no more honey-penned introduction to the river and its landscape than that with which Wilde starts his happy volume, which is so incomparable that it bears repetition here in full:

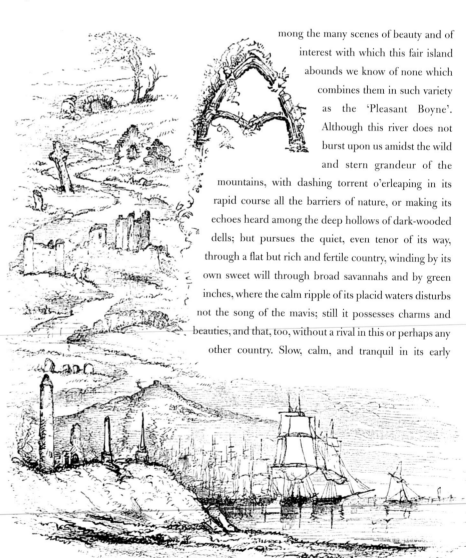

mong the many scenes of beauty and of interest with which this fair island abounds we know of none which combines them in such variety as the 'Pleasant Boyne'. Although this river does not burst upon us amidst the wild and stern grandeur of the mountains, with dashing torrent o'erleaping in its rapid course all the barriers of nature, or making its echoes heard among the deep hollows of dark-wooded dells; but pursues the quiet, even tenor of its way, through a flat but rich and fertile country, winding by its own sweet will through broad savannahs and by green inches, where the calm ripple of its placid waters disturbs not the song of the mavis; still it possesses charms and beauties, and that, too, without a rival in this or perhaps any other country. Slow, calm, and tranquil in its early

Fig. 1: The decorative initial A on the first page of William Wilde's The Beauties of the Boyne *(1849) was accompanied by a sinuous drawing showing what you can expect to see if you follow the river from the source to the sea.*

course, the mower whets his scythe in the deep meadows by its brink, and the reaper gathers the corn from the very margin of its waters; the swift and the martin skim over its clear surface, and the robin sings in the ancient thorn that rises out of the adjoining hedgerow. The very mayfly, as it lights upon it, breaks the mirror of its surface. The wide-spreading circles which make the springing of the trout, or the timid breathing of the roach, are all, save the flapping of the water-hen, or the easy paddle of the baldcoot, that disturb its placid bosom.

In this gentle stream there is no inequality – no roar of waters nor spray of cataract; it is not boisterous nor yet sluggish; neither broken by the sudden rapid, nor calmed spreading into the broad lake; but, pure and undefiled, it springs from the crystal fountain of the living rock – its source sanctified by religious veneration, and commemorated in legend and in song; serene and peaceful, like a true philosopher, it glides noiselessly on, in deep but calm repose, bestowing the blessings of fertility on the counties through which it flows; bearing on its bosom the intercourse which socialises man; enriching, beautifying and civilising, it receives in return the homage of its tributaries, and finally mingles with that eternity of waters, the sea. Winding through the heart of the ancient kingdom of Meath, green homesteads, picturesque villages, peaceful hamlets, and thriving towns rise on its banks; the hand of man has turned its power to good account, and mills and factories draw their animation from its waters; the freights of foreign lands, the luxuries of far-distant countries, are borne on its stream towards the interior, and the produce of our own soil and the industry of our people is carried downwards on its tide. Deep hanging woods and rich plantations of noble parks and extensive demesnes, where the willows dip into its calm waters, and the oaks and elms of centuries are mirrored in the wave beneath, stretch for miles along its course, where

Slow, and in soft murmurs, nature bade it flow.

Towards its centre, and as it nears the sea, its banks become more elevated, their outline more picturesque. Here, rising abruptly from the water's edge, their castled crags, bending over the stream, remind us of the scenery that characterises the Rhine between Cologne and Mayence; in other places, sloping gradually from the river, their sides are clothed with foliage of the deepest, darkest green, piled up in waving leafy masses to their very summits, so that the sun itself is hidden (except at noon) in many places from its dark waters. The summits of many of these verdant banks are crowned by ruins of castles, towers and churches, feudal halls, and high baronial keeps, still noble even in their decay, and forming, as they are cut clear and sharp against the azure blue beyond, pictures in the landscape, unsurpassed in grace and beauty by any in the land. In the broad lawns that here and there interpose between these verdant banks and steep o'erhanging precipices, we find the noble mansions of some of the highest of our nobility, and many of the most memorable ecclesiastical remains – the cell of the hermit, the cloister of the monk, and the cross of the pilgrim – that Ireland, rich as she is in relics of the past, can boast of. Ancient stone circles, massive cromlechs, and numerous green mounds, raised by our Pagan ancestors, some clothed with velvet sward, but others fringed with young plantations, are thickly interspersed among the more attractive objects that catch the eye, as it descends upon the limpid surface of the Boyne. Highly cultivated lands, richly ornamented seats, and a population, generally speaking, more comfortable, more intelligent, and more advanced in civilisation than the majority of our peasantry, may fill up the outline we have faintly and briefly endeavoured to draw of the general characteristics and present appearance of this celebrated river; and though Spenser has not sung its praises, nor Raleigh gossiped upon its banks, it has been hallowed by events the most interesting in our country's annals. So memorable in ancient history, and so rich in monuments of the past is it, that we fear not to assert that the history of Ireland might be written in tracing its banks. Many a broad smiling plain through which it flows, now green with waving corn, or perfumed and decorated by the wild flowers of a pasture land, or by some delicate female hand cultivated into the elegant garden, in the bowers of which the birds of spring are singing, was once the scene of mortal strife, and crimsoned with the blood of warriors, where the clang of battle, the shout of the victorious, the groan of the dying, and the prayer of the suppliant, alone were heard. Scarcely a ford upon this river but was disputed in days gone by; every pass was a Thermopylae; the bardic annals teem with descriptions of its battles; the fairy lore of other days yet lingers by its tranquil waters; and scarcely a knoll or mound, or rock, or bank in its vicinity but still retains its legend.

We would do well to start here by following Wilde's footsteps from the source to the sea, for the basic elements of his narrative still remain the same – the landscape and the legends, the tombs and tributaries, the castles and the churches – not to mention the canals, the bridges, the mills and the weirs. But things have changed very much, too, since Wilde's day. The mower whetting his scythe is no longer with us, the lesser branch railway lines now sleep without sleepers, the mill-wheels are silent and the pleasure-boats have long since stopped bringing tourists upstream to Beauparc. The hum of the bees has been replaced by the sounds of jets and juggernauts; carts have become cars; tractors, not horses, pull ploughs; the thatched cottages of the poorer folk have largely made way for the bungalows of a much more prosperous land; hedges have been felled to make larger fields; and the countryside is reduced by the ribbon development of expanding towns.

In addition, academic research has come on in leaps and bounds. Excavation, particularly in the Bend of the Boyne below Slane, has provided us with much more information about our past than Wilde could ever know, and the proliferation of valuable archaeological and historical journals, both local and national, has yielded up so much more detail about people and places that a whole new picture emerges over and above what Wilde presented to his readers.

It is all of these considerations that make it desirable to look at the Boyne Valley anew, to retrace his steps in following its course geographically from where it rises, near Carbury, to where it discharges itself into the Irish Sea, at Mornington. In one respect, however, we shall not be accompanying Sir William, and that is in exploring the Boyne's most important tributary, the Blackwater, which joins it at Navan: this book is specifically about the Boyne itself. We shall, nonetheless, include places located on or near some more minor tributaries, and be a little naughty in straying as far afield as Duleek, which is on the Boyne's smaller sister river, the Nanny. Culturally and historically, Duleek fits in neatly with the Boyne Valley – and it was also, incidentally, included by Wilde, who cunningly left out the course of the Nanny on the map at the end of his book.

The Boyne Valley, more than any other area of comparable size in the country, has a series of monuments of various kinds that provide an unequalled cross-section of what Ireland's past has to offer in terms of its built heritage. Even more, these monuments – be they prehistoric Passage Graves, monastic High Crosses and Round Towers, medieval castles and abbeys, or spacious country houses – are among the best in the country, providing us with an ideal backdrop for the panorama that is Irish history. Thus, in addition to Wilde's horizontal view of the Boyne as it flows from start to finish – given an updated treatment in the first half of this book – I shall also provide what the archaeologist would see as a vertical stratigraphy from bottom to top so as to provide a chronological framework for the various happenings and monuments in the valley. I shall hand-pick the cherries, choosing good examples to help illuminate and link together the last five thousand years from prehistory to our own times – though it should be noted that the nineteenth and twentieth centuries, being relatively close to our own day and lacking the venerable antiquity of the earlier material, do not play a very prominent role in the narrative.

The quality of these monumental treasures of the Boyne Valley are such that they can serve as a microcosm not only of the counties which the Boyne touches or flows through – Kildare, Offaly, Meath and Louth – but also of the entire country. The richness of the soil in the lands bordering and drained by the Boyne is what provided the wherewithal down the centuries to create these extraordinary monuments, and it is that very extraordinariness which makes the Boyne Valley so special, so different from other areas of Ireland.

The very uniqueness of the Boyne Valley makes it eminently worthy of a volume which goes beyond Wilde's to bring out in text and picture the highly individual character of what the region has produced down the centuries – not just stone monuments but also artefacts and works of art that should be treasured. I hope that I succeed in helping you to appreciate those treasures all the more through bringing them together in description and illustration between the two covers of a single book.

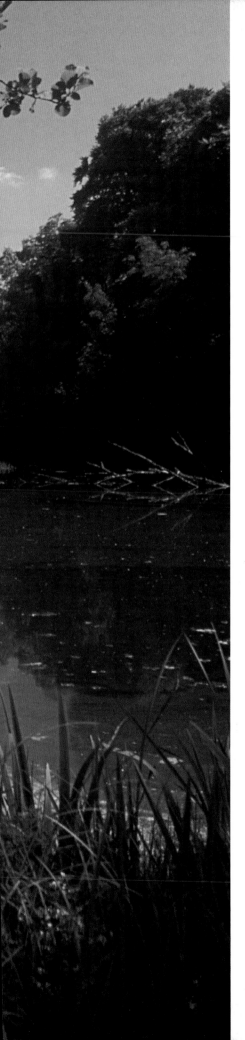

Chapter 1

The Boyne from the Source to the Sea

The Source and Carbury Castle

The Boyne is traditionally said to rise at a well located in the grounds of Newbury Hall, near the foot of the Hill of Carbury, and dedicated to the Trinity. As Sir William Wilde pointed out, however, the well is fed by a stream which comes from marshy ground somewhat to the north of Carbury village, and which, in turn, supplies water to a beautiful lake nearby (fig. 2). Nevertheless, it is the well itself which gave rise to the ancient story as to how the river came into being. According to this tale, there was a prehistoric King of Leinster named Nechtan who had a well in his garden that would blind anyone who approached it other than the king and his three cup-bearers. The curiosity of his queen, Bóann, was aroused by this, and she determined to test the mystical powers of the well itself. She was able to thwart its curse by walking around it three times to the left (i.e. widdershins). No sooner had she done so, however, than a spring rose up, and out of it three enormous waves came over her, making her blind in one eye and pushing her ahead of them towards the sea where, along with her faithful lapdog Dabilla, she was swept to her death in the foamy brine. But her body must have been rescued, for she is said to have been buried somewhere in the great cemetery of Brú na Bóinne (see page 114).

Her husband, Nechtan, is also something of a shadowy figure, and probably originally a water-deity. The Hill of Carbury, overlooking the

Fig. 2: Water from the well forming the source of the Boyne flows directly into this lovely lake in the grounds of Newbury Hall in County Kildare.

source of the Boyne, was anciently called Sidh Nechtain, the fairy hill of Nechtan, suggesting that he must have had some connection with the Otherworld. On the undulating surface of the hill are a number of mounds, and it comes as no surprise that some of these, excavated by G.F. Willmot in 1936, turned out to contain prehistoric cremation burials. Included in the finds were a number of stone flints dating back to the Stone Age, showing that the origins of Carbury Hill go back many thousands of years.

It is no wonder that people were attracted to this hill, for it rises majestically above the Bog of Allen in west Kildare and east Offaly, and is lord of all it surveys for many miles around. Wilde enumerates Dublin, Kildare, Meath, Carlow, Westmeath, Longford and Offaly as the counties to be seen from it, and it provides a wonderful panorama over the plain to the hills of southern Leinster, far away to the southeast. Even more eye-catching is the imposing castle which tops its brow, giving it a more imperious look than the other hills visible on the surrounding skyline.

The name 'Carbury' comes from that of the Gaelic family Ó Ciardha, or Keary, said to have descended from Niall of the Nine Hostages – one of the first Irish kings to emerge from the mists of Irish prehistory – and who were the owners of much of the land hereabouts. But their 'red-bladed swords' were not enough to keep the recently arrived Normans from taking over the place in the twelfth century – at first the FitzHenrys and later the de Berminghams. The strength of the castle that we see today, which is later in date, is explained by its closeness to the edge of the Pale – the region of Norman-dominated territory, its boundary ever-changing. The castle thus acted for centuries as a bastion against the native Irish resistance to the take-over of their territory, and Carbury was often at the centre of a tit-for-tat war of attrition and domination.

An earlier castle had been rebuilt in 1447, but Red Hugh O'Donnell demolished it and laid waste the area in 1475. The Irish stormed the renewed castle in 1546, whereupon King Henry VIII's Lord Justice devastated much of the neighbouring county of Offaly. That part of the castle looking westwards and keeping a weather eye out for native Irish

'marauders' may well be the oldest part of the whole complex of buildings; although now much dilapidated, it is shown in watercolours of the 1770s by Gabriel Beranger (fig. 3) as looking like a late-medieval tower-house with, for defensive purposes, only few and small windows.

The really imposing portion of the castle looks southeastwards. This later part was probably begun when one Henry Colley, alias Cowley, was granted a 21-year lease of the castle and manor in 1538, which lease was renewed in 1569. This section rises up defiantly above the hill, a sheer face of stone punctured on the first and second floors by windows that still bear traces of the subdividing mullions and transoms typical of the period. Each of the floors had a number of different rooms, some provided with fireplaces; the corresponding chimneys are octagonal and very tall, dominating the skyline. One of the fireplaces on the top floor still bears traces of decorated stonework, and we can imagine the Colleys, dressed in opulent Elizabethan garb, looking from the windows over the plain which stretched out below to the blueish hills of south Leinster in the distance.

In 1570, Henry Colley was appointed Seneschal of the Barony of Carbury, which enabled him to assemble the inhabitants in defence of the county and to banish or punish all malefactors, rebels, 'idlemen' (vagabonds) and rhymers or harpers. Knighted in 1576, he died in the mid-1580s. He was married to a daughter of Sir Thomas Cusack, a rich Meath landowner, parts of whose family tomb survive in the church on Tara Hill. Henry's son, Sir George Colley, did even better in marriage: his wife was a daughter of Adam Loftus, Archbishop of Dublin and first Provost of Trinity College, Dublin.

And that is not the end of the family fame. In 1728, Henry's descendant Richard Colley became heir to the property of his first cousin, Garrett Wellesley of Dangan in County Meath, on condition that he and his heirs assume the surname and arms of Wellesley. Thus Arthur Wellesley, later to become none other than the Duke of Wellington, was not really a Wellesley by blood but a Colley. We shall encounter the Iron Duke again later, when the river reaches Trim.

By the mid-eighteenth century the castle was owned by two Colley daughters, neither of them apparently beauties but with a sufficiently adequate fortune for them to be able to get married. One of these, Elizabeth, wed a Mr Glover and later moved to London; she was responsible for taking the roof off the castle and thereby making it uninhabitable. The other, Maria, married a Pomeroy in 1747, and may have been responsible for building the fine mansion of Newbury Hall in the 1750s on ground that once belonged to the castle – and in the grounds of which is the Trinity Well, popularly seen as the source of the Boyne.

It is from this humble beginning in a small well, where patterns or annual local pilgrimages used to take place on Trinity Sunday, that the Boyne starts its 113 km course to the sea, during which journey it falls only some 88 m. From something quite minuscule, the stream grows into a large river, sluggish at first but picking up momentum as it goes along – although the water-speed varies, of course, depending on the time of year. It can lay claim culturally and historically to being 'the most famous river in Ireland'.

At the Boyne's other end, at Millmount in Drogheda, near where the river finally meets the sea, there is a museum containing one of the four surviving examples of a kind of vessel that was used on the Boyne, mainly for salmon netting. This is a coracle, almost square but with rounded corners, and illustrated here (fig. 4) from a modern reconstruction in the Brú na Bóinne Centre. Coracles were made of wicker and covered with animal hide (in more recent centuries canvas had been substituted for the hide). The coracle is a cousin of the rather larger currach or *naomhóg*, still very much alive up and down the west coast of Ireland. For fishing it needed two people, one to paddle at the bow and the other to deal with the nets. Canon Cyril Ellison, in his valuable book *Waters of the Boyne and Blackwater: A Scenic and Industrial Miscellany* (1983), points out that it was used also to ferry people across the river – in which event, presumably, one fisherman made way for a passenger.

So let us now get into our coracle and quietly drift down the river – at least partially in the company of Sir William Wilde, the first page (see fig. 1, page 10) of whose book gives us a visual inkling of what we are likely to meet en route. We will for certain meet a number of weirs, but in that case we can do what a French visitor once described seeing a Boyne fisherman do when a storm threatened: namely pull to the bank, turn over the coracle, put it above his head, and walk to beyond the weir – in the process keeping the rain off as well.

Fig. 4: A modern reconstruction of the kind of coracle used for fishing on the Boyne from time immemorial is on display at the Brú na Bóinne Interpretative Centre.

Edenderry and the western end of the Boyne

We normally think of 'the Bend of the Boyne' as that area where the great Passage Grave cemetery of Brú na Bóinne is located, a few miles below Slane. But even before the river begins to gain momentum here, it has expanded into a much larger bend at its western extremity, for it starts flowing westwards before making a great curve – which forms the southwestern boundary of the lily-white county of Kildare – and then heading eastwards. Having arisen in the shadow of the Hill of Carbury, it flows towards a second hill, now occupied by the town of Edenderry – one of only a comparatively small handful of Irish towns formed around (if not actually on) a hilltop. This hill, too, is occupied by a castle, but, although solidly built, a far less imposing one – just three storeys, and without a single vault. The castle was built by the Blundell family which, through marriage, had come into possession of Carbury Castle by 1650. Theirs is the name attached to the aqueduct, a kilometre and a half south of the town, that carries the Grand Canal across the road to Rathangan. Nearby, a broad spur of the canal goes right up to the foot of the southwestern side of the hill, and the townspeople have been very assiduous in cleaning it all up and making the canal-side walk along the old towpath into a proud local amenity.

Again through marriage, the Edenderry property in due course passed to the second Marquess of Downshire, of Hillsborough in County Down, whose opposition to the Act of Union in 1800 cost him dear but raised his standing in the eyes of his Irish tenants. For them, he built the town's central feature, the Corn Market-cum-Town Hall; this was burned in the 1940s but, after various vicissitudes, was restored and reopened as a Town Hall in 1998.

Being blocked by the hill, the Boyne flows around the northern perimeter of the town, where it acts as the boundary between the counties of Kildare and Offaly. As already mentioned, during the later Middle Ages this area served as the border of the Pale, that area of eastern Ireland where Anglo-Norman writ ran. It is for this reason that the region is puckered with castles, not just Carbury and Blundell castles but a host of others in the locality as well. One of these is Carrick Castle, located along with a medieval church on a hillock some four kilometres north of Edenderry. The full name was Carraig Fheorais, 'the rock of the de Berminghams', the family that built the castle. *The Annals of the Four Masters*, among others, report that in 1305 Sir Pierce Mac Feorais (alias de Bermingham) invited the Gaelic chieftain O'Conor Faly, together with his kinsmen Maelmora and Calvagh O'Conor, to a banquet in the castle and, with Jordan Comin, massacred them as soon as they rose from the table, along with twenty-four of their Irish followers. In a Remonstrance to no less a person than Pope John XXII, this slaughter was cited as an instance of treachery by the English visited upon their Irish neighbours. Not even de Bermingham's arraignment before the English king could bring any apology from him, or any justice to bear on the matter. No wonder, then, that de Bermingham has gone down in Irish history as 'the treacherous Baron' – though it should be added that the de Berminghams, under their Gaelic name Mac Feorais, became in due course 'more Irish than the Irish themselves', and actually joined up with a later generation of O'Conor Falys against the English in County Meath.

Only 3.2 km southwest of Carrick Castle is yet another de Bermingham fortress, this time called Kinnafad: a large and rather chunky tower-house whose windowless walls create something of an interior gloom. It stands close to what was once a ford across the Boyne – still shallow enough here to be passable – and so its protective function is easily understood.

The Boyne Valley

Many's the fight must have taken place around here over the ages, for, when the river was being dredged and straightened in the nineteenth century, a considerable number of weapons – daggers, spearheads and swords – as well as axes, dating from prehistoric times to the earlier Middle Ages, were rescued from the mud. These formed the prize exhibits in a private museum of antiquities formed by Thomas R. Murray of Edenderry and later acquired by the University of Cambridge Museum of Archaeology and Ethnology around 1900.

Less than one and a half kilometres to the north-northeast, and less than five kilometres northwest of Edenderry, is yet another tower-house. This is Grange, which must surely be reckoned among the jewels at the western end of the Boyne (fig. 5). It was built in the fifteenth or sixteenth century by the Tyrells. The tower has tall Elizabethan/Jacobean angular chimneys, but its most unusual and striking feature is the Dutch gable-style battlements – a subsequent addition, perhaps made as late as the 1640s. In front of the tower is a charming single-storey eighteenth-century stone house with a coat-of-arms above the door. To one side is a courtyard flanked by farm buildings. The whole complex, together with the adjoining garden, makes an enchanting group, and is an unexpected delight to encounter on a quiet country road in west Kildare. The family that built and lived in it until the nineteenth century has now set up the Tyrrell Trust which, along with Dúchas and others, has been restoring the castle to a high standard. Chancing upon this little gem has been one of my highlights in preparing this book.

The junction of counties Kildare, Offaly and Westmeath is where the Boyne is joined by the Yellow River, which itself has a tributary, the Castlejordan. This latter is doubtless called after the village of the same name, which has an interesting collection of two castles – with unusual rounded turrets – as well as an early-nineteenth-century church. The castles are further evidence for entrenchment on the outskirts of the Pale.

But let us return to the Boyne where, less than three kilometres west-northwest of Edenderry, there are the remains of a Franciscan friary called Monasteroris Mac Feorais (the latter part of the name comes, once more, from the Irish name adopted by the de Berminghams). The friary was founded by Sir John de Bermingham in 1325, a mere eight years after he had defeated the Scottish King Edward Bruce at Faughart in County Louth. It was fortified by the O'Mores in the sixteenth century and, remarkably for its comparatively diminutive size, is credited with having withstood a siege by Queen Elizabeth I's Lord Deputy, the Earl of Surrey. It served as a Protestant parish church until 1777, when divine service was moved to the new church built near the Blundell Castle in Edenderry; and in both places there are memorials to Father Mogue Kearns and Colonel Anthony Perry, who were hanged at Edenderry for their part in the 1798 Rebellion. The church is now divided up into a number of separate family vaults, over the doorway of one of which there is an inscription lamenting the death of a lady named Marian, daughter of Colonel Newton and affectionate wife of Henry Clarke of yet another castle at Ballybrittan, 'who fell asleep in Jesus while repeating the Litany in the House of the Lord' at the age of 33.

With the extra water from the Yellow River, the Boyne now begins to grow in size and emerges into a landscape which, unlike the low-lying land through which the river has hitherto navigated, has small hillocks on either side. On the river's right are Rahin Wood and Russellswood. The increased flow and width of the river can best be appreciated in the long straight stretch visible from Ballyboggan Abbey, which stands close to the Meath bank.

Fig. 5: The charming tower-house with decorative battlements, recently refurbished, dominates an attractive eighteenth-century house at Grange in West Kildare.

Fig. 6: The keen eye can spot these two grimacing faces high up on the south-eastern corner of the medieval abbey at Ballyboggan, Co. Meath.

Ballyboggan Abbey seems at first sight like a long, dull and interrupted rectangular box of masonry, but a walk down the elegant avenue of trees from the roadside reveals that the building does have interesting features. It was once a long hall-church, but closer inspection shows that it had a north and south transept which were lit with tall, slender lancet windows. Windows of this same shape were used at the east end in a cluster to form a five – or more probably seven – light window, through which the sun must have shone in vertical strips during morning services. This arrangement was replaced in the fifteenth century by a single broad window, and it was probably in the course of the same alterations that two curious grimacing masks (fig. 6) were carved high up on the southeastern corner of the church. The western block of masonry is remarkable for the number of putlog holes it has; these would originally have held the beams of scaffolding when the church was being built, and for some unknown reason were never filled up.

The windows indicate that the oldest part of the structure dates from the thirteenth century, when the abbey was founded for the Augustinian Canons, allegedly by John Comin; though the historian James Ware maintained, by contrast, that it owed its foundation to some unnamed Englishman in the twelfth century. Certainly it remained for the three centuries of its activity an English-dominated monastery, although in 1399 an Irishman, one John O Mayller, was 'instituted' to the priory against the dictates of the Statutes of Kilkenny, which forbade Irishmen getting control of monasteries such as this. Prior John did not last long, however, and the *status quo* was restored when one Richard Cuthbert proved that he was really the lawful prior.

It was perhaps a fire that led to the partial rebuilding in 1446 of the chancel and the insertion of the single east window. When Ballyboggan was surrendered to the king at the Suppression of the Monasteries in 1537, it was said to have owned 5,000 acres, and the very next year the 'Holy Cross of Ballboggan' – obviously a much venerated relic – was 'burned by the Saxons'.

Three years later, Sir William de Bermingham was created Baron of Carbrie and granted the monasteries of Ballyboggan and Clonard. These he may have felt were his just rewards for having attended a Parliament in Dublin the previous year which had abolished papal jurisdiction in Ireland, transferring it to King Henry VIII – an occasion allegedly accompanied by great rejoicings in the capital city, with free wine for the citizens among bonfires and illuminations and a general amnesty for all gaolbirds. On Sir William's death in 1548, a fine effigy was carved of him in the full panoply of his so-called 'white' armour; this effigy, together with some of the tomb-surrounds, is preserved in a small chapel at Dunfierth, not far from Johnstown Bridge in County Kildare.

The road from Ballyboggan to our next port of call passes Ticroghan, where a small information plaque informs the passer-by of the former presence in the neighbouring field of a once formidable stone castle. All you can see now are low earthworks, but inspection of the terrain, particularly when aided by a glance at the six-inch Ordnance Survey map, reveals that those earthworks have corner bastions, shaped (when seen from above) like spearheads, of a kind best known from Charles Fort in Kinsale, County Cork, which was built somewhat later, around 1680, and in stone. The outer defences at Ticroghan were probably, like many of the same period, designed as earthen fortifications from the very start; and it had a square interior protected by those spear-shaped bastions at the corners. These may have been erected around the 1640s, though the fort bears the name of Queen Mary, who preceded Elizabeth as Queen of England in the previous century.

The castle was certainly one of Owen Roe O'Neill's midland garrisons in the 1640s. His son Henry had married Elena, daughter of Sir Luke FitzGerald of Ticroghan. Owen Roe had come back from France to help the 'Catholic' armies of the Confederation of Kilkenny to regain Irish land and rights from the English King Charles I. His main supporter in Ireland was the Earl of Ormond, who was actually stationed at Ticroghan when his arch-enemy, Oliver Cromwell, was attacking Drogheda, with the disastrous results we all know about (see page 86).

Cromwell's two generals Hewson and Reynolds closed in on Ticroghan and captured the defences in 1650. The castle was then under the command of Sir Robert Talbot, a kinsman of the FitzGeralds; he had hoped in vain that Lord Castlehaven would come to relieve it. Wilde tells the story that the Cromwellians were about to give up their siege when they noticed that the garrison guns were firing bullets of silver. Realising that the defenders

Fig. 7: Not a stone survives of the romantic castle at Ticroghan, shown here in a watercolour of c. 1779 by Gabriel Beranger after an original drawing by Thomas Ashworth, now preserved in the Special Collections of the Library of University College, Dublin.

must be doing this as a last resort, the Cromwellians persisted and soon took the fortress, which they then retained for at least a year.

An eighteenth-century drawing by Thomas Ashworth, as copied in watercolour by Gabriel Beranger, shows how imposing a fortress this once was, with towers of stone inside the earthern fortifications that could have acted as an admirable model for a romantic Walt Disney film set. Presumably during the last quarter of the eighteenth century, or even later, wreckers in search of building stone must have found the castle a ready-made quarry and finished the demolition which the Cromwellian siege-guns had begun. As we look at Beranger's watercolour (fig. 7) we realise that, in terms of ancient monuments, Ticroghan represents one of our greatest losses along the whole length of the Boyne.

Clonard to Donore

The nearby monastery of Clonard, which will be discussed again below (see page 137), is not strictly speaking on the Boyne, but it can be included here because of its close proximity to the river. Indeed, the stained-glass window in the north transept of the Catholic church in the village says that it illustrates an angel calling on St Finnian to found his monastery by the Boyne. This window is one of a series in the church executed in 1957 by Billy Hogan to show various events in the saint's life, while the two wooden statues of St Finnian and St Etchen which flank the altar were carved in Italy. But this mid-nineteenth century Catholic parish church is not on the site of the ancient monastery, and nor is the nearby white Carrara marble roadside statue of the saint, which was carved in Italy by Carlo Nicoli and placed in its present location in the same year that the stained glass was inserted in the church, 1957. The only connection between the modern church and what is taken to be the site of the old monastery – and it is a somewhat tenuous connection at that – is the fine baptismal font (see fig. 92, page 136) located today behind the high altar. A plaque at the back of the Catholic church records that this font was brought to its present location on 1 October 1991, having been removed from the now deconsecrated Church of Ireland church, only a kilometre away, which is thought to stand on the site of the ancient monastery.

The Church of Ireland structure, which has not been used for some years, dates only from the early nineteenth century, when it replaced one that seems to have been more fortification than church and dates perhaps from the fifteenth century. On the far side of the bridge here across the small Kilwarden River is a tree-topped motte (fig. 8), token of the Norman presence even before Simon de Rochfort became bishop of the see of Clonard in 1192.

Fig. 8: The motte near Clonard is one of the earliest reminders of the presence of the Normans in County Meath.

Fig. 9: The figure of a queen, dating from the late twelfth century, is the only known survivor of a set of ivory chess-pieces found in a bog near Clonard. It may be of Scottish or Scandinavian origin, and was possibly brought to Clonard by someone in the retinue of Simon de Rochfort, bishop of Clonard. It is now in the National Museum in Dublin.

The rivers and bogs around Clonard have delivered up a number of objects of which at least some were probably associated with the early Christian monastery. These include fragments of a crozier and a house-shaped shrine, and also a well-preserved wooden bucket, decorated with bronze, which probably was used for holy water during liturgical ceremonies. A single ivory chessman (fig. 9) has survived from a set that must have helped while away the time of monk or knight in the twelfth or thirteenth century. The objects are now preserved in the National Museum in Dublin.

At Edenderry we encountered the Grand Canal (see page 19), which had reached the upper reaches of the Boyne before 1800; after the turn of that century the Royal Canal came to compete with it, crossing the Boyne just south of Longwood. It is only when you walk along the old towpath for the horses that pulled the boats and barges, and then get down off the canal bank to the old ground level, that you realise just how enormous the works were that made it possible. Vast quantities of earth had to be transported to raise the canal to the level of safety above the surrounding bog; where a dip occurred – as when the canal had to cross the Boyne – sizeable bridges had to be built.

Ruth Delany, author of the major book on the Royal Canal, *Ireland's Royal Canal* (1992), echoes early-nineteenth-century opinion when she says the Boyne aqueduct is the finest of its kind in Ireland (fig. 10). Out in the middle of peaceful countryside stands a tall bridge with a large single span supporting the canal, which narrows slightly as it crosses some 20 m above the Boyne. Building the aqueduct was quite some achievement, and the cost of this enormous project must have added to the Royal Canal Company's financial problems as it strove to link the Shannon to the Irish Sea.

As it was to prove, the canals were not able to compete with the speed of the railways built across the midlands in the mid-nineteenth century, and duly succumbed. The railway companies often bought out the canals so that they might use the adjoining land to build their tracks, as is the case here. There is something sad and symbolic in seeing both canal and railway running side by side, the rapid railway almost thumbing its nose at the laggardly pace of the canal. However, the canals are now coming into their own again: they are being restored, and offer tremendous recreational facilities for both boater and walker as a wonderful way to get away from the hustle and bustle of modern speed transport.

Before reaching the aqueduct, the Boyne has already been crossed by the Leinster Bridge on the Dublin–Galway road. The current bridge was built in 1831, apparently to replace an older one which had become unsuitable for the amount of coach-traffic using it.

The Boyne itself has picked up both speed and depth by the time it goes under the aqueduct, and here it can flow untrammelled because of the extensive drainage which took place in the 1970s, leaving characteristic long piles of mud snaking along the banks.

Below the aqueduct, the river is joined from the left by another tributary, the Deel, just above Inchamore Bridge. Here the Boyne passes under the watchful eye of Donore Castle (fig. 11), a small tower-house in state care which has rounded corners, a vaulted ground floor and a rounded turret for a staircase at the corner beside the door. Old maps show a chapel and Dominican friary close by, suggesting that the castle was part of a whole medieval settlement complex. It has become far better known than its size would warrant in consequence of the fact that H. G. Leask, in his 1941 book *Irish Castles and Castellated Houses*, chose it as a typical example of what is known as a £10 castle. In 1429, King Henry VI offered a grant of £10 to any liegeman of his who would build a castle to a minimum of 20 ft in length, 16 ft in breadth and 40 ft in height to defend the Pale, whose movable – and often invisible – boundary lay between the areas of English rule and those where the Gaelic Irish were doing what they could to avoid such rule. The dimensions of Donore conform roughly to the measurements specified in the Statute, and there is nothing against accepting it as a £10 castle since it may have been built, as required, within ten years of the offer being made. Other castles in Meath, Westmeath and Louth probably fit into the same £10 category too. (The grant was probably undersubscribed, as a similar offer requiring somewhat smaller dimensions was made some years later.)

After Donore, the Boyne starts to change course in order to weave its winding way through low-lying territory that will lead us to its first large town, Trim. The river heads northwards from Donore, then eastwards under Scarriff Bridge before turning northwards once more to go under Derringdaly Bridge. Finally, before it reaches Trim it turns eastwards again, past Newhaggard, where, only a little more than a kilometre west of Trim, there is an interesting cluster of buildings including a large two-storey Georgian house, an impressive six-storey battlemented mill, and a medieval tower facing it across the river.

Of this trio, the tower is the most unusual, because it does not conform to our usual notions of what a late-medieval tower-house should be. It forms a long rectangle, vaulted on the ground floor and with a projecting stair-tower on the southeastern corner enabling

Fig. 10: The water of the Royal Canal (top right) is borne high above the River Boyne (bottom left) on a aqueduct near Longwood that is regarded as one of the finest examples of early nineteenth-century canal architecture in the country.

Fig. 11: The late-medieval tower-house at Donore stands sentinel above the Boyne and is considered to be one of those ten castles encouraged by the Government of the time to guard the English Pale in the fifteenth century.

access to (originally) two floors above. Other than the vaulted arch, which ran from end to end until the southern end was blocked up, the most remarkable feature of the tower is, at the northern end, the machicolation above the arch's level, carried on six corbel brackets. The existence of the machicolation – through which boiling water, arrows and the like could be despatched – suggests the necessity of defence against attackers coming from the direction of the river. The tower has all the appearances of being a gate-house guarding an access from the banks of the Boyne – but access to what? There is no other large castle behind it, nor are there any signs of a stone building to which it might have acted as an entrance, although comparable towers not far away at Liscarton and Moymet led to a castle and church. Perhaps here at Newhaggard is an instance of some important Boyne buildings having quite simply disappeared without trace.

At Tremblestown, little more than a kilometre to the northwest and adjoining the river of the same name – which flows into the Boyne near Newhaggard – is another example of a castle and a medieval church, although the latter has virtually disappeared. But this small tributary has something much more peaceful and colourful to offer in the form of one of County Meath's finest gardens, Butterstream, a little over a kilometre west of Trim (see pages 37–38).

Trim and environs

The waters of the Boyne have been flowing under the bridge at Trim for many centuries. We know from *The Annals of the Four Masters* of the existence of a bridge at Trim as far back as 1203. James Grace's *Annals of Ireland* tell us that in the year 1330 there was a great flood, especially of the Boyne, in consequence of which, with one exception, all the bridges on that river were carried away, 'and other mischief done at Trim and Drogheda'. From this we can conclude that the present four-arched bridge is of later date, and Peter O'Keeffe and Tom Simington in their detailed book on Irish bridges, *Irish Stone Bridges: History and Heritage* (1991), believe the existing structure was built not long after that great flood. This may also have been the same bridge for which, in 1425, the king ordered money to be paid to the Archbishop of Armagh.

The bridge probably stands on the site of the old ford from which the town gets its name, Ath-truim. The solid rock on which the piers are perched was exposed during the Boyne Drainage Scheme in the 1970s, when the riverbed here was lowered by 1.2 m. The bridge serves to join two parts of the town which each preserve interesting medieval remains that make Trim – along with Adare, Kilkenny and perhaps also Fethard in County Tipperary – one of the most interesting medieval towns in the whole country.

Though no less a man than St Patrick is said to have left St Lomman in charge of a church here, Trim did not really begin to come into its own until 1172. The story of de Lacy's castle will be told elsewhere in this book (see page 160), but the town that grew up around it, and under its protection – particularly on the opposite side of the river – must rapidly have become so large that it needed enclosing by stout walls, entered through a total of five gates. Only one of these gates – the Sheep Gate – survives, standing somewhat forlornly on the north side of the river in the middle of a very large field to the east of the landmark Yellow Steeple. As was also the case at Drogheda (see page 163), the walls fortified considerable areas on both sides of the river, probably from fairly early on in the town's history and – in the view of Avril Thomas, author of the comprehensive book *The Walled Towns of Ireland* (1992) – at latest by the first half of the thirteenth century. Because the Boyne would have been navigable for shallow-draughted boats at least up as far as Trim (and probably beyond), we may presume that there was a harbour between the two unequal portions of the town, located on the northern flank of the castle.

In the early centuries of its existence, Trim was a very prosperous town, containing not only Ireland's strongest castle but also a number of – presumably wealthy – religious houses within its walls. One of these was the Cathedral (see below). Another was St Mary's Abbey, of which the Yellow Steeple was the tower and which had been in existence before Hugh de Lacy ever set eyes on the place. The Franciscans had a house where the old courthouse now stands, but more affluent was that founded for the Dominicans by Geoffrey de Geneville (d.1314), a thirteenth-century successor of Hugh de Lacy as Lord of Meath, and who entered the monastery himself as a friar in 1308. When de Geneville did so he entrusted the lordship to his grandson-in-law, Roger de Mortimer (1287–1330), whose descendants bequeathed the town and its buildings to Richard Plantagenet, Duke of York; upon the latter's death in 1460 it became the property of the Crown.

In a memorandum written to the Lord High Treasurer in 1584, the parson, Roger Draper, recommended Trim – a place 'full of very faire castles and stine houses builded after the English fashion and devyded into five faire streets' – as the most suitable place for the first Irish university; only eight years later Dublin's Trinity College was founded,

Fig. 12: Air balloons glide majestically over the misty Meath landscape above Trim.

Fig. 13: In fields near Trim, the Yellow Steeple of St Mary's Abbey looms dramatically above the tingling winter frost.

thus beating Trim to it. Trim was to remain a flourishing market town throughout the following three centuries but, by the nineteenth century, Navan, farther downstream, began growing at Trim's expense, leaving Trim to remain (fortunately for us) comparatively undisturbed ever since.

One of the oldest sites in the town is the Protestant Church of Ireland Cathedral, northwest of the bridge; its position may reflect the location of St Lomman's original church foundation. The current church itself dates from no earlier than 1801, and was renovated in 1869; but the tower through which it is entered goes back to the fifteenth century. The chancel which belonged to the medieval church stands immediately to the east of the present building; it bears carved heads of a king and a bishop on the label stops of a window inserted in the sixteenth century. The construction of this medieval church is normally attributed to Richard Plantagenet, Duke of York, whom we have just met; he had inherited lands in Trim in 1427, and lived here for a while in 1449. A font formerly in the chancel and now in the church dates from the fifteenth century; it bears the Royal Arms of England and those of James Butler, the White Earl of Ormond, suggesting that here again the Duke of York may have been putting his hand in his purse to help create it.

Even more interesting are the medieval fragments in the porch. These presumably came from the earlier church on this site. Of considerable importance is the unusual slab with a male and female head and a Crucifixion; John Hunt dated this to the second quarter of the fourteenth century, and it is one of the very few representations of the Crucifixion to survive from that century anywhere in Ireland. There is also an unusual decorative screen-fragment from Ardbraccan bearing the figure of a bishop, but the finest piece of carving is the top of a pinnacle bearing the figures of six apostles, showing the high quality of craftsmanship prevalent in this area during the fifteenth century.

Trim's skyline is dominated by the spire of the nineteenth-century Catholic church of St Patrick, on the south side of the river, and the Yellow Steeple (fig. 13), to the north. The latter, one half of one of Ireland's most elegant medieval towers, was aptly described by Sir William Wilde as 'the guardian genius of the surrounding ruins'; the other half, it is averred, was demolished by Oliver Cromwell, the scope of whose destructiveness as perceived in Irish tradition probably far outweighs the damage he actually caused. The Yellow Steeple has stepped string-courses outside. The seven storeys within rise to a height of 38 m, which must have given the peal of its bells a tremendous range across the Meath countryside – not to mention affording a grand view for those with enough breath and vigour to climb to the top. The tower belonged to the Augustinian Abbey of St Mary which – like the Cathedral – had patrician associations and was rebuilt a number of times, the steeple being probably a thirteenth-century construction. During the Middle Ages the abbey was famed above all for its miraculous statue of the Virgin, known as Our Lady of Trim, which must have brought affluence to the monastery by way of the many pilgrims who came to venerate it. Like the cross at Ballyboggan (see page 23), Our Lady of Trim was burnt by Reformation zealots in the late 1530s.

Close by is Talbot's Castle (fig. 14), a private residence with a garden sloping down to the Boyne, close to the bridge. *The Buildings of Ireland* volume on North Leinster (1999) by Christine Casey and Alistair Rowan maintains, however, that it may once have formed the refectory of the Augustinian priory or abbey, pointing out that a report of the Commission for Irish Education in 1827 described it as 'a very old building forming part

Fig. 14: Once owned by Jonathan Swift's beloved Stella, Talbot's Castle high on the banks of the Boyne was also where the Duke of Wellington and the mathematician and Astronomer Royal, William Rowan Hamilton, went to school.

*Fig. 15: Arthur Wellesley,
later the Duke of Wellington,
spent much of his youth
at Dangan and in the
environs of Trim.*

of the quadrangle of St Mary's Abbey'. In the interval between its original construction in the fifteenth century and the time when it was converted into a private house, around 1909, it had served, among other things, as a diocesan school, originally for a mere fourteen day-boys but later for boarders.

Perhaps the school's most famous pupil was none other than the Duke of Wellington (fig. 15), whose family, as we have seen, were really the Colleys (or Cowleys) of Carbury Castle. He spent his youth at Dangan, some five kilometres south of Trim, and his nurse claimed that he was born there – although his mother, who surely knew best, said he was born in Mornington House in Dublin's Upper Merrion Street. By a curious quirk of fate, the young Arthur Wellesley was born in the same year, 1769, as his grand French imperial adversary, Napoleon, whom he defeated on the fields of Waterloo in 1815.

The famous Mrs Mary Delany (1700–1788), who visited Dangan on a number of occasions during her two marriages, liked the place less and less as time went on; she remarked on the garden having a vast man-made lake six hundred yards long, complete with islands, a fort with 48 cannon, and a complete twenty-ton model of a man-of-war, so the place sounds more conducive to nurturing a budding admiral than a future general! All of this aquatic landscaping had taken place long before Arthur Wellesley was born.

In an interesting article in *Ríocht na Midhe*, Vol. IX (1994/95), Elizabeth Longford says that, as a pupil here, Wellesley was quick at mathematics, and that he was unhappy when taken away from his school at Trim to further his education in Dublin. He had a literally high-flying cousin, Richard Crosbie, who made Ireland's first balloon ascent – from Dublin in 1785 – and another from Limerick in the following year. Crosbie's aspiration to heights led him to climb the Yellow Steeple, a feat sufficiently foolhardy to encourage him to make a will before starting the climb; when he returned safely to the ground

Fig. 16: William Rowan Hamilton, the brilliant mathematician and exponent of quaternions, went to school in Trim, where his uncle was headmaster. His portrait hangs in the Royal Irish Academy in Dublin.

he is said to have found his young cousin Arthur in copious tears because Richard had left him nothing in his will.

Commemorated by a Thomas Kirk statue on a column erected in the town by his Meath admirers, Wellesley started off as simple Captain Wesley before being knighted and becoming, in succession, Chief Secretary for Ireland, conqueror of Napoleon and Prime Minister of Britain. Before scaling such heights he had been elected a Member of Parliament for Trim. During his two-year tenure of the seat he apparently did not utter a single word in the House, although he was forceful enough outside it to prevent the Freedom of Trim being bestowed on poor Henry Grattan, who had won Ireland's parliamentary independence in 1782.

Mathematics may have been a strong point at the school, for another famous pupil shone in that particular branch of learning: William Rowan Hamilton (1805–1865), whose formula for the multiplication of quaternions, written on a Dublin bridge of the Royal Canal, opened up great new perspectives in the world of mathematics and brought him fame and the post of Astronomer Royal (fig. 16). Hamilton's headmaster was his Uncle James, who would occasionally take him on trips around the countryside in his carriage. After one of these, at the age of 17, he wrote the following lines:

And now behold me as away I dash
Guiding the reins and flourishing the lash.
Boyne's silent banks we startle as we pass;
Its placid surface, like to polished glass,
Gives back the light of noon without its glare,
And diamond sparkles deck its bosom fair.

The Boyne Valley

We leave the town and ruins far behind,
New prospects opening and new scenes we find . . .

(from Robert Graves's *Life of Sir William Hamilton*, Vol. I)

While a boy at Trim, Hamilton developed his own semaphore system, and he used the Yellow Steeple as a giant gnomon for a huge sundial he created. It is of course as Ireland's greatest mathematician that we know him best, but, as the verses just quoted show, he was quite capable of tossing off poems at the slightest provocation. One of the longer ones was 'Verses on the Scenery and Associations of Trim', of which we may quote the following lines here:

Yet lovely all the prospect seems,
And suited to a poet's dreams.
O'er all the verdure of the scene
Fresh sunbeams fling a brighter green;
Clouds of every shape and dye
Are scattered o'er the deep blue sky;
And melody of many a bird
In the charmèd air is heard.
Through those boughs so closely twining
The river's sparkling waves are shining;
Adown its course, the little bays
Are glittering in a fuller blaze;
And as by fits the gentle blast
So fondly o'er the bosom passed
Of the bright Naiad in repose,
Saw you not how new beauties rose?

How well with this surrounding bloom
Contrasts those ramparts' solemn gloom!
With what a proud and awful frown
Appear their turrets to look down
On all beside that meets my gaze,
On monuments of later days,
On all that modern art around
Has reared upon this classic ground!
O genius of those ruined towers,
Who lovest to dwell in ivy-bowers,
Have I not paid thee honour due;
Have I not kindled at the view
Of thy majestic walls, surveyed
While the meridian sun has stayed
His steeds above them, or his light
At morn or eve illumed their height,
Or bright Orion from above,
Or that fair Vesper, star of love!

Have I not watched the stealing shade
When moonbeams on thy summit played,
While sound or motion there was none,
Except that stealing shade alone:
And thought within those massy walls,
In those so long deserted halls,
Nobles and warriors sat of old,
Clad in refulgent arms and gold,
Arrayed with hauberk and with helm,
And gave their laws and ruled their realm?
Their bones have mouldered in decay,
Thy greatness hath not passed away!

(from Graves, *op. cit.*)

An actual owner of Talbot's Castle who had links with a much more celebrated poet was Esther Johnson, better known as Stella, who bought it for £65 in 1717 and sold it the following year for £200 to her admirer Jonathan Swift, who felt there was no better place to take the country air than Trim. Stella used to stay in Trim with her seemingly uninspiring companion Mrs Dingley when Swift was in residence at Laracor, three kilometres to the south, where he had been presented to a living with a sizeable income in 1700; only when he was away would she stay in his parsonage. On his first arrival, Swift found both his house and the church to be rather dilapidated, and an 1852 drawing of the former in *The Illustrated London News* shows how uninspiring the residence was anyway. Swift loved going to Laracor, however, and wrote to Stella that 'riding to Laraghcor gives me short sighs as well as you', adding in 1711 that his journeys thither did him 'more good than all the ministries these twenty years'. He set about improving the place, adding twentyfold to the acreage he owned and creating a Dutch-style canal, where he planted cherry and apple trees, a grove of hollies and double rows of willows, and seems to have enjoyed a bit of eel and pike fishing too.

Swift's efforts to introduce a weekly prayer-service on Wednesdays met with no success, as he often found himself preaching only to his clerk rather than to any of his fifteen-strong congregation. In time, he left the care of his parishioners to a curate, though he retained the living for himself until he died in 1745. He never forgot Laracor, however, endowing the church with tithes he had bought himself. As a man who always gave a third of his income to the poor, Swift ensured in his will that those tithes should pass to the poor of Laracor in the event of the church being disestablished (which, 135 years after his death, it was). Despite his efforts, today 'all is ruin once again': nothing remains of his gardening activities or even of his church and residence. The successor church, built in 1855, has been deconsecrated and is no longer used for ecclesiastical purposes.

Swift's time at Laracor was written up in the fifth volume of *Ríocht na Midhe* (1972) by Jim Reynolds. In Reynolds, the Dean has found something of a horticultural successor in the area, for, at Butterstream, a little over a kilometre or so west of Trim on the Kildalkey road, Reynolds has created a canal of sorts, a long open stretch of water which is the spiritual link between Swift's Laracor, the Boyne only a few hundred yards away, and a superb garden (fig. 17, page 38) which he has developed over the last twenty years. He was given a patch here by his father where he could try his hand at growing roses, but a visit to

Fig. 17: The magical garden created by Jim Reynolds at Butterstream near Trim is a tranquil haven of peace amid a blaze of ever-varying colour during the spring and summer months.

the garden created at Sissinghurst in Kent by Sir Harold Nicolson and his wife, Vita Sackville-West, inspired him to create his own, which, as at Sissinghurst, embraces an old, low country house. Reynolds was happy to repay his horticultural debt to England in 1995 when he received Prince Charles and showed him proudly around the garden.

The garden is carefully designed to be a clever mixture of the formal and the natural. One focal point is a lawn overlooked by conifers, flanked by a classical portico and adjoined by a summer house where the mallets are kept for the occasional game of croquet of a summer evening. The potted plants which ooze out onto the grass include a *Fuchsia magellanica versicolor* of a lighter green than that which proliferates on the Kerry roadsides and the largest boxwood of its kind, which hails from the Azores. The garden seems never to end, giving unexpected glimpses into hidden nooks and crannies around every corner. Anyone visiting the garden between April and September is bound to find riots of different colour depending upon what the spring, summer or autumn has brought. It is easy to realise why *The Good Gardener's Guide* awarded Jim Reynolds its highest two-star accolade for having created this Boyne-side gem.

Even with St Patrick's Cathedral, St Mary's and the Yellow Steeple, Talbot's Castle, the Wellington monument, the castle, Laracor and Butterstream, Trim is not yet at an end . . . Despite other, more recent, fine architecture, such as the façade of the former gaol, looking towards the castle, our view is inevitably directed downstream to the medieval ruins of Newtown Trim, which will be discussed in greater detail elsewhere (see page 166). Clearly visible from the upper floors of Trim Castle, and once reachable from it along a medieval roadway, the Cathedral and Abbey of Saints Peter and Paul at Newtown Trim is, when seen from the river, an imposing pile by any standards, the putlog holes in its western part being rather reminiscent of those at Ballyboggan (see page 22). For anyone looking at the monastery not from the Boyne but from across the Boyne, it is worth stopping for a moment at what is known as the Echo Gate and hollering over to the domestic buildings of the church – only to find, if the noise of traffic allows, a splendid echo of one's own voice returning.

Just to the east of the old cathedral is a smaller structure, doubtless an old parish church, which contains a single jewel: the limestone tomb-chest of Sir Lucas Dillon and his wife Jane Bathe, of Moymet (see page 168). He is accoutred in renaissance armour and rests alongside his wife on a cushion, both with their hands on their breasts. On the long, western side of the chest we can see the whole family: Sir Lucas and Lady Jane flanked (as so often on late-sixteenth- and early-seventeenth-century tombs) by all their children, above whom are written the words 'Deus' and 'God'. The coats-of-arms on the long sides are those of the couple, together with the arms of Sir Lucas's second wife, Marion Sharl. The empty shield at the eastern end presumably contained the inscription, recorded in Lodge's *Peerage of Ireland* for 1789, telling the world in Latin hexameters that Sir Lucas, Member of the Privy Council and Chief Baron, passed to his eternal reward at the age of 64. Even though 17 February is given as the day of his death, no year is given. The tomb was probably erected sometime around the early 1590s, during his lifetime, and the inscription may well have been painted on after he died in 1595. This is undoubtedly the finest Elizabethan monument in the whole of the Boyne Valley, and one which has withstood the elements remarkably well over the last four hundred years, much of which it must have spent reclining in the open air.

Just downstream from the Cathedral and the Dillon tomb, the Boyne flows under yet another medieval bridge (fig. 18), this one so narrow that it needs traffic lights to control the single line of cars and lorries that can pass over it. Over a quarter of a century ago the local authority considered widening the bridge, but wisely decided instead to build the modern cement structure you can see farther upstream, beside Trim Castle, thus leaving this splendid hump-backed bridge much as it was when first built over half a millennium ago. Its creator was perhaps William Sherwood, Bishop of Meath from 1460 to 1482, who, on what we may take to be its completion around 1475, cleverly rented it off to the Crown. It has five well built arches, with upstream cutwaters, one of which rose to parapet level to

Fig. 18: An engraving by George Petrie of around 1820 shows cattle going for a paddle in the Boyne above the medieval bridge at Newtown Trim, with the Priory of St John in the background, where the Crutched Friars ran a hospital to care for the sick.

Fig. 19: The Boyne flows slowly eastwards to greet the warm glow of the early morning sunrise at the Priory of Newtown Trim.

offer a small refuge to protect pedestrians from speeding carriages. In their book *Irish Stone Bridges: History and Heritage*, O'Keeffe and Simington were of the view that this bridge was more substantially built than the one at Trim, although the latter would probably have been of far greater importance.

Just below the bridge, on the southern bank, is yet another complex of Newtown Trim buildings. These once formed the Priory of St John (fig. 19), built for a community of what were known as the Crutched Friars because of the cross (Latin *crux*) they bore on the fronts of their habits. They were a branch of the Augustinians, but devoted themselves specifically to serving the sick, including some who were probably indeed on crutches. In short, this complex was a hospital, and the buildings that survive, at the northwestern corner beside the bridge, may have been the wards, their running water being supplied by the Boyne, which flowed down towards them.

The adjoining church was built originally in the thirteenth century and, like the Cathedral of Saints Peter and Paul just upstream from it, probably by Simon de Rochfort. It was altered in the fifteenth century, with a rood screen and gallery being placed at the junction of nave and chancel, a spot now marked by a solitary pillar-base which formed part of the structure – a rare survival, as only two other examples of such rood screens are known from Ireland.

The tall towers, which are visible from a distance, all date from around the fifteenth century. They comprise: a tall sacristy adjoining the church; what were probably the prior's quarters, with their back to the bridge, and a lone building, standing by itself at the southwestern corner, which may have acted as a guard-tower. The excavator David Sweetman, working in 1984, discovered many shards of medieval pottery but also a number of seventeenth-century wares, suggesting that the care here of Meath's sick outlasted Henry VIII's closure of the monasteries in the years after 1536.

Bective area

Over a kilometre downstream, at Scurlogstown, the Boyne is joined from the right by the Knightsbrook River, which makes it change course northeastwards. From this junction onwards downriver there used to be a number of instances where a medieval church and castle were nestling close to one another beside the Boyne, but time has dealt harshly with them.

Not a trace remains of the castle of Scurlogstown, a mighty tower-house with rounded turrets and corners illustrated by Sir William Wilde (and also in Vol. II of Thomas Cromwell's 1820 book *Excursions through Ireland*), nor of the mill close by. Even the church is a rather characterless remnant of its former self, though what was probably a Norman motte survives forlornly near the riverside.

The same general fate befell the church and tower-house at Trubly, three kilometres or so downstream; the last remnants of the tower-house here were blown down in a storm in the 1970s. The castle at Trubly was similar to that at Scurlogstown, according to Wilde, who tells us that Cromwell slept in Trubly the night after the siege of Drogheda, and that his cannon balls are traditionally said to have caused a crack in one wall of Scurlogstown Castle, whose foolhardy occupant had dared oppose him.

It is only a little more than a stone's throw downriver from Trubly before the Boyne goes under yet another notable bridge, this time beside the abbey (fig. 20) at Bective (discussed

Fig. 20: The drama of the sky unfolds over a wintry scene at Bective Abbey.

Fig. 21: Undeterred by
frozen banks turned white
with snow, the Boyne flows
seawards below Bective Bridge.

*Fig. 22: One of Ireland's
greatest exponents of the
short story, Mary Lavin
grew up at Bective to become
the Boyne's most articulate
and sensitive prose writer
of the twentieth century.*

*Fig. 23: The genial Lord
Dunsany, himself an
imaginative writer, was
quick to spot the talent of
Mary Lavin and Francis
Ledwidge – all together,
a remarkable literary
trio nurtured close to
the banks of the Boyne.*

in some detail on page 169). The nine-arched bridge (fig. 21, pages 42–43) looks very medieval, but as no reference to it has ever been found earlier than 1821, its date – even approximately – remains a mystery.

The bridge gave its name to the first published volume of one of Ireland's best-known and best-loved short-story writers, Mary Lavin (1912–1996), whose *Tales from Bective Bridge* first appeared in 1943 (fig. 22). After arriving from America, where she had been born and spent her early childhood, Lavin lived with her family at Bective, and thereby gave the Boyne Valley one of its most important literary voices. Early in her career, she was a protégée of another Meath author who, unlike her, has been going through a period of undeserved oblivion. This was Lord Dunsany (1878–1957), described by Edward Power in *The Irish Times* of 23 March 2002 as a fantasist who wielded an inestimable influence over the evolution of speculative fiction in the twentieth century, his wistful fantasies representing 'a vibrant link between ancient myth and modern speculative writing'. Dunsany (fig. 23) played host to Yeats, Kipling, Lady Gregory and St John Gogarty at his castle at Dunsany, only a few miles away. He is well remembered today for his championing of not one, but two great Meath writers, which is summed up in the opening of the Preface he penned for *Tales from Bective Bridge*:

> I have had the good fortune to have many stories and poems sent to me by young writers. In nearly all of them the ardours of youth showed flashes, some rarely, some frequently, but only in two of these have I felt sure that I was reading the work of a master. And these two great writers, as I believe them to be, both wrote to me by a strange coincidence from the same bank of the same river, the left bank of the Boyne. One of these writers was Francis Ledwidge, who unhappily lived too short a time to do much more than show promise of the great bulk of fine writing of which I am sure he was capable. But, although he has not a very large number of readers, that early promise of his has received the recognition of lovers of poetry, both in his own country and at the ends of the earth.
>
> I have now the pleasure of introducing another fine writer, Miss Mary Lavin; very different from Francis Ledwidge, except for the same piercing eye, which to Ledwidge revealed the minutest details of Irish hedgerows, with all their flowers and birds, and to Mary Lavin the hearts of women and children and men.

This feminine quality of hers to probe into the feelings and 'hearts of women and children and men' comes out in a story entitled 'Asigh' that appeared in *Memory and Other Stories* (1972). It tells of an only daughter and 'the long imprisonment of her life' with a father whose beating of her with a buckled strap has brought on an ulcer that has ruined her marriage prospects. Her brother's main pleasure is 'scything through the weeds and the wild grasses' down by the river's edge, where 'the corncrake made himself heard with a harsh sound'. Descriptions such as these were probably inspired by the banks of the Boyne.

The title of the story is the name of a place just a kilometre and a half downstream from Bective Bridge. Like Scurlogstown and Trubly, Asigh had a castle and a church, but once again not a trace remains of the castle, while the church is disintegrating at the centre of a little churchyard in a very large field. One of the sixteenth-century rectors of Asigh (or Assey, as it was then called) was Henry Ussher (*c.* 1550–1631), who lies buried where his family had owned the neighbouring townland of Balsoon since the thirteenth century. He was to go on to become one of the founders of Trinity College, Dublin, and later

Archbishop of Armagh. His son James (1581–1656), who succeeded him as Archbishop of Armagh, is the Archbishop Ussher famous even today for his 'calculation' of the date of the Creation: 4004 BC. Sometime around 1590 Henry built a tower-house for himself at Balsoon, the vaulted ground floor of which – complete with well-preserved wicker-shuttering – still survives under a grassy mound in the grounds of the nineteenth-century Balsoon House.

The character of the Boyne's surroundings begins to change at Scurlogstown. Instead of having comparatively flat banks on either side, the river begins to make a deeper bed for itself as the adjacent countryside gradually starts to rise around it. By the time the Boyne has reached Bective Bridge, the slope down to the riverbank has begun to get steeper, and Bective Abbey, with the splendid beech tree which casts its shadow on the building's southwestern corner, seems to be all the more elevated above the river – the very height of the structure only helping to emphasise this elevated status.

As the river continues downstream from Bective (fig. 24), the banks become even steeper and more wooded, in particular with the beech trees in the grounds of Bective House. The extent of the gradient can be measured by the railway bridge at Asigh, now disused and private property, which must be about 12 m above the riverbed; it once served the line going from Dublin and Clonsilla to Navan, which it reached in 1858.

The same steep slope, particularly on the southern bank, is very much present in the grounds of Bellinter House, now run as a conference centre by the nuns of Our Lady of Sion. The house (see page 182) is an excellent and little altered example of the style of the architect Richard Castle or Cassels. The view from its front door looks past what must be one of Ireland's most splendid weeping beech trees towards the Hill of Tara, which forms

Fig. 24: The river expands as the banks grow gradually higher between Bective and Bellinter Bridge.

*Fig. 25: Old and new trees
mingle in the frost below
Bellinter Bridge, where the
river turns northwards.*

the elevated skyline in the distance, and is discussed in further detail on pages 125–33. It was that ancient royal residence, Tara, which provided the title for the Preston family, who built Bellinter House when they were raised to the peerage. We find the name of John, Lord Tara, inscribed on Bellinter Bridge, just a little below the house and bearing the date 1813, when it was erected.

More recent tree-plantings lead to a stretch of river where the Boyne turns northwards (fig. 25) and then northwestwards past Ardsallagh in its gradual approach to Navan. It was the 'noble demesne of Ardsallagh' which led Wilde to wax lyrical as follows:

> In no part of its course does the river present the same extreme calmness and repose as here. Widening into deep, still pools, shaded by aged timber, and fringed with wild plants of gigantic growth; huge colts-foot, with the modest blue forget-me-not and the little yellow potentilla peeping through their dark umbrageous foliage; long, toppling bulrushes, fragrant meadow-sweet, and broad water-lilies, stretch in wild luxuriance along the placid banks. Long avenues of lime trees, and groves of tall grey-stemmed beeches with arcades of aged yew, give an air of antiquity as well as grandeur to this handsome park.

The gardens of the original Ardsallagh House (replaced by the present structure in the 1840s) had already been much admired a century before Wilde's encomium when visited by Swift and his lady correspondent Mary Delany, who recorded that she was delighted by the garden dug low near the river 'and so well crowned with trees of all kinds that nothing could be more wilder or romantic'.

Not far away, and a kilometre away from the Boyne's banks here, is the small medieval church of Cannistown, dedicated to St Brigid, who also has a holy well near Ardsallagh. Though possibly built on the site of a monastery founded by St Finnian of Clonard in the sixth century, this is more likely to have been a new foundation by the Norman family of de Angulo (later anglicised to Nangle) in the period around 1200. It is a small nave-and-chancel church with a doorway in the north wall. Its main feature is the thirteenth-century chancel arch, which is supported by slender pillars and rather abraded foliate capitals. Standing on these are two sculptures that form the base of the arch itself. The one on the south side has a curious animal hunt among foliage, while the one on the north side has a carving with three figures who, though often taken to be enacting the Arrest of Christ, are unlikely to be doing so because they can be seen to be sitting at a table. On this table are five small containers, so an alternative interpretation of the scene is that it is the Marriage Feast of Cana; however, weathering makes it impossible to determine any satisfactory identification. In the wall above the carvings are corbels, probably from the fifteenth century. That on the right bears three cat-like heads holding up a stone carved with a figure holding a book, while the corbel on the other side, which seems to represent the veiled head of a woman, in turn carries a stone above, also carved with a human figure, whose two hands are facing in the same direction. All of these images are as mysterious in their intent as the earlier carvings of the chancel arch. The church was obviously considerably altered in the fifteenth century (to which also belongs an arch attached to the back wall), and what remains of the east window looks as if it could be yet another alteration, this time from no earlier than the sixteenth century.

Fig. 26: The recent stained-glass windows of George Walsh in the Catholic church at Johnstown near Navan are among the most exciting of their kind in the whole Valley of the Boyne. The parish priest, Father Nicholas Dunican, guided the choice of subjects depicted.

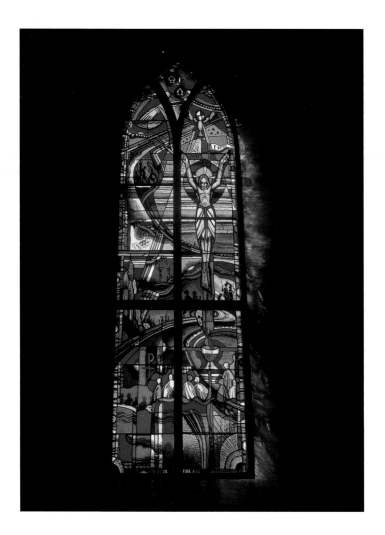

Navan area

The medieval period is represented in a rather different way in a surprise church at Johnstown, on the opposite (eastern) bank of the Boyne. The surprise is the wonderful impression of multi-coloured brightness you get on entering the church, the result of a number of remarkable stained-glass windows (figs. 26–27), done by George Walsh in 1999–2001, which reach almost from floor to ceiling. The whole effect makes this one of the most interesting Catholic churches along the whole length of the Boyne.

Built into the outer eastern wall of the porch is a carving of a small figure of a cleric, standing on a pedestal; this was probably originally a part of the cloister arcade of Bective Abbey (see page 173) or at least carved by the same hand or produced by the same workshop.

Close to the altar of the church is a squat but attractive baptismal font, dating from about 1500, divided into twelve niches, one per side. Ten of these are occupied by single apostles and an eleventh by a squashed pair of apostles. The final one unusually illustrates the Coronation of the Virgin, a scene borrowed perhaps from some medieval English alabaster. This font was regarded as being of sufficient quality and significance to be brought to Dublin in 1853 for display in the Great Exhibition on Leinster Lawn. It did not originate in Johnstown, however, having been buried in the seventeenth century, probably near Kilcarn on the other side of the Boyne, to avoid destruction by iconoclastic

Fig. 27: Around the large-scale chalice, the stained-glass artist George Walsh introduces a fascinating array of small narrative figure-groupings in the Catholic church at Johnstown. His windows illuminate the Paschal mystery of the Passion, Death and Resurrection of Christ.

zealots, only to be subsequently exhumed and placed in the old church there before finally making its way here.

To have got to Johnstown, the font must have crossed Kilcarn Bridge. Described by Christine Casey and Alistair Rowan in the *North Leinster* volume of the *Buildings of Ireland* series as 'among the finest late-medieval bridges to survive in North Leinster', this has four central arches flanked by three smaller ones on one side and four on the other. Probably built in the second half of the sixteenth century, its upstream side was later extended, so that only the downstream elevation, with its original cutwaters, preserves something of the pristine appearance of the bridge. It was closed to traffic in 1977 when a modern concrete replacement was opened upstream.

We encounter only one further bridge – a railway viaduct – before we reach Navan, the second-largest town on the Boyne. Navan owes much of its modern prosperity to the lead–zinc mines on the northern side of the town, which are among the largest of their kind in Europe. Sir William Wilde complained that the inhabitants of Navan turned their backs on the Boyne; their houses looked inward, away from the river, with only a few of the narrow streets providing even a glimpse of the Boyne or the Blackwater, which join together here. However, particularly on the sunny southern side of the town, things have improved markedly since Wilde's day.

Navan's old Irish name, Nuachongbhail, was retained even after the Normans took over the area, and their baron, de Angulo, built the motte on the western end of the town, close to where the railway now is. The motte was in danger of destruction half a century ago, but good sense prevailed to preserve what is Navan's oldest surviving monument, dating from the last third of the twelfth century.

Street names such as Trim Gate indicate that the town was walled during the medieval period; a stone on the exterior of Ryan's Pub proclaims 'Trim Gate' on one face while on the other it says that this part of the town wall 'was rebuilt April ye 19th 1786'. By that time most of the old walls had probably already been demolished, thus opening up the town to further development.

While 1786 may have been the last time the walls were rebuilt, it was certainly not the first. Their best-known reconstruction was after a disastrous raid on the town by Con O'Neill and Manus O'Donnell in 1539, when Navan was a border outpost of the English-dominated Pale. *The Annals of the Four Masters* report that on this occasion the victors obtained immense and innumerable spoils on the expedition when they utterly plundered Navan – which was, therefore, obviously not just a fortress but an important market town. One symbol of this status was its Market Cross, of which a portion is now preserved in the National Museum in Dublin. As if by way of exchange, a fragment of a cross from Nevinstown (between Navan and Rathaldron) is now on display in the Meath County Library at Navan. Its inscription, in Latin, states that Cusack, Knight, and Margaret Dexter, his wife, had the cross made in the year 1588. One can imagine the masons chiselling away at the inscription oblivious of the fact that, elsewhere, the Spanish Armada was running into terrible difficulties as it rounded Ireland in storms that would ensure most of the sailors would never see home again.

In more recent times Navan lost other treasures that once belonged to it, namely the two silver maces (fig. 28) of the town which, as Canon Cyril Ellison's excellent book *Waters of the Boyne and Blackwater: A Scenic and Industrial Miscellany* (1983) tells us, became part of the collection of the famous US news magnate William Randolph Hearst in California, and were then given by him to the Los Angeles County Museum of Art. However, by good fortune and the efforts of John Bruton and the late John Teahan, they have now returned to Ireland, being preserved in the National Museum's Collins Barracks building.

One treasure the town does still have (though one suspects it is not fully appreciated by all of those who gaze upon it) is a wooden figure of the crucified Christ (fig. 29), with finely modelled musculature and a flowing loincloth. This is set on the background of a cross that hangs above the high altar of St Mary's Church in the town centre. It is important as the earliest known – although already mature – work of Edward Smyth (1749–1812), who was probably born in the town. Smyth went on to become Dublin's most famous sculptor, carving large statues on the Custom House and the Four Courts for James Gandon, who described him as 'an artist capable of the highest works of art, either as a modeller or a sculptor'. For our purposes, his most relevant carving is the head on the south face of the Custom House representing the River Boyne and bearing the date 1690, referring to the Battle of the Boyne (see page 82), but also bedecked with sheaves of wheat representing the agricultural richness of the sculptor's native county of Meath. His father is reported by one source to have been a stone-cutter, and Edward may have belonged to a dynasty of talented craftsmen in stone, as he was possibly a descendant of the H. Smith who is recorded on the Balrath Cross (see page 177) as the person who carried out the work of beautifying it in 1727.

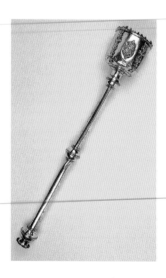

Fig. 28: This silver mace was made by Andrew Gregory in 1680–81 for the Corporation of Navan, and would have been borne in procession before the Portreeve, Burgesses and Freemen of the town. Recently repatriated from California, it is now in the Collins Barracks section of the National Museum in Dublin.

Fig. 29: The figure of the crucified Christ hanging above the altar of St Mary's Church in Navan is one of the earliest known sculptures of Edward Smyth, a native of the area who went on to carve great statues for the Custom House and Four Courts in Dublin.

Another famous family associated with Navan were the Beauforts. The first to have associations with the town was Daniel Cornelis Beaufort, who arrived from a Huguenot church in London in 1747 to become rector of Navan, where he wrote a treatise entitled *A Short Account of the Doctrines and Practices of the Church of Rome, Divested of All Controversy*. His son, Daniel Augustus Beaufort (1739–1821) succeeded his father as rector in 1765 and was later installed as Vicar of Collon in County Louth, where, as an amateur architect, he built the beautiful perpendicular-style church modelled on the chapel of King's College, Cambridge. An early member of the Royal Irish Academy, Daniel Augustus is best remembered for his map of Ireland, which he published in 1792 along with an accompanying memoir indexing all the places marked on the map and placing them in their appropriate parishes and baronies – a remarkable feat that made the map a true forerunner of the work of the Ordnance Survey and the Townland Index. David Augustus's son Francis Beaufort (1774–1857), later a knight and rear-admiral, is even better known worldwide for having established the Beaufort Scale of wind force. He did this pioneering work after being appointed Hydrographer to the Royal Navy, a post that 'rendered his name almost a synonym in the navy for hydrography and nautical science', according to *The Dictionary of National Biography*. He was a brother-in-law of Richard Lovell Edgeworth (father of Maria), and with him established a line of telegraphs from Dublin to Galway.

Fig. 30: The actor Pierce Brosnan, a famous son of Navan, and now an Honorary O.B.E.

In more recent times, Navan has proudly boasted of another native son who has become a star on the world stage: the actor Pierce Brosnan (fig. 30), perhaps best known for his film roles as James Bond.

The town of Navan may once have had a castle, if not two, and it is quite likely that one would have stood near the confluence of the Boyne and the Blackwater, the advantageous geographical feature that gave the town its strategic and economic importance – although Navan's only bridge seems to have been the one over the Blackwater, which bore the road from Kells and northwestern Meath. In the same way that the Knightsbrook River makes the mighty Boyne change its course at Scurlogstown, so the addition of the Blackwater causes the Boyne suddenly to change from a northerly to an easterly direction before, shortly afterwards, it turns towards the northeast, where it once more forms a valley, beautifully wooded on either side.

Where the Boyne twists sharply to the right at the junction with the Blackwater lies the suburb of Athlumney, on the road to Kentstown. It is dominated by Athlumney Castle (discussed in more detail on page 174), which formed part of a whole medieval manor that included also a Norman motte and a medieval parish church, both on the far side of the road. The church is now a ruin, but is worth visiting for the grimacing stone head (fig. 31) carved high up on the side wall of the belfry, looking out over the motte.

Fig. 31: This wrinkled stone face looks out hauntingly from the wall of the ruined medieval church at Athlumney, a suburb of Navan.

The Blundells built a flax mill close by in 1806, beside the Boyne, and exploited the riverside location to ship out the linen. With the decline of the linen trade, the mill was converted in 1907 to woodworking, and later again, according to Canon Ellison, to the production of furniture and saw-milling. What had been built as an 'indestructible' mill fell a victim to the flames of a disastrous fire in 1933. Nevertheless, Navan is still to the fore in the production of furniture.

Also in Athlumney is Ruxton Lock, the first of a number of locks we will meet along the next stretch of the Boyne, between Navan and Slane. This provides an appropriate opportunity to introduce the Boyne Navigation into our narrative. The intention of the Boyne Navigation was to increase trade along parts of the Boyne by providing a canal beside the river which could help boats overcome the weirs that made commercial traffic impossible. The idea had begun to take shape in the early years of the eighteenth century, but it was not until the middle of the century – 1748 to be precise – that any construction began, working upstream from Drogheda. The company that was formed aspired to make the Boyne navigable as far up as Trim, as must have been the case in the Middle Ages, but, while some money was spent on improvements in the upper reaches, Navan was realistically as far as the Navigation ever got (see fig. 33, page 54).

Most of the initial operations concentrated on the stretch up to Slane, where the Jebb Mill was extremely active in producing flour which was easier to transport downriver to Drogheda, at the mouth of the Boyne, than overland to Dublin; from Drogheda it was exported to England and as far away as Bordeaux. David Jebb, member of a Drogheda family of Nottinghamshire origin, was architect, builder and manager of the Slane mills, and he became engineer, secretary and treasurer to the Boyne Navigation Company. His two interests became inextricably linked, and, were it not for the needs of the Slane mill, it is doubtful if the Navigation would have made the progress it did.

Canon Ellison quotes a report of 1792 to the effect that 'all locks are nearly completed and the Navigation from within half a mile of Navan to the town of Drogheda is at this time capable of navigating vessels of upwards of 20 tons burden' – the words 'within half a mile of Navan' probably referring to the Ruxton Lock beside Athlumney, completed in 1792. Certainly by 1800 at the latest, cargoes of coal, wheat, culms and small amounts of timber and slates were reaching Navan, with the downstream cargo including flour, oats, barley, yarn and linen.

By the end of the nineteenth century, a steam barge named the *Ros na Ríogh* had been built to bring tourists up the river, as photographs in the Lawrence Collection can visually document (fig. 32). A tour was organised that combined boat with road and railway travel – which latter would ultimately put the Boyne Navigation out of business, as it did also the

Fig. 32: A hundred years ago, the tourist could take a leisurely trip upriver from Oldbridge to Beauparc aboard the SS Ros na Ríogh (shown here in a Lawrence Collection photograph in the National Library), and then return home by train in the later afternoon.

Royal and Grand Canals. Boyne Valley Development Tours produced a pocket-size guidebook for a penny in 1903, from which Canon Ellison quotes the following:

> The water trip Drogheda to Slane and back is a new departure in the development of the Boyne Valley. A steam launch leaves Oldbridge daily at 10.45 during the season for Slane, travelling through some of the most beautiful scenery in Ireland. The celebrated caves of Newgrange are passed and can be visited by arrangement. The boat arrives in Slane in time for lunch at the hotel Boyneville [see page 74] at one o'clock . . . If time permits, the launch should be engaged to proceed to Beauparc at 2 p.m. Visitors will be astonished at the treat in store for them on this part of the river; it cannot be surpassed for fine views and foliage throughout the entire run.

The same brochure advertised Fulham's famous bicycles, made in Drogheda, Healy's celebrated mineral waters and a souvenir silver spoon available from H. Harbinson of West Street in the same town!

By 1915 the canal's finances were in severe decline, and the whole Navigation was bought over by the Navan millers John Spicer & Co., still happily with us. In 1961 much

Fig. 33: The Ramparts at Navan are part of the Boyne Navigation which created the Boyne Canal and bridges to link the town by boat with Drogheda and the Irish Sea.

of the canal was handed over to An Taisce, the Irish National Trust, as a public amenity – a generous gesture which helped provide a wonderful riverside walk from Navan to Drogheda now called the Boyne Way.

The canal switched from one side of the river to the other as the local topography demanded, and the horse pulling on the towpath on one side was taken aboard the barge or lighter and transported to the other side, where it would continue its weary drag. But where the Boyne Way starts, just below Navan, the canal is all on one side. (The walk is accessible also from the road at a number of other points.) Here the river can become quite broad and fast-flowing, rolling majestically through beautifully wooded countryside, often with the banks quite steep on both sides. A lovely little green area (adjoined by a car park) at Athlumney introduces us to the first lock – like all the others, this one is no longer operational. Beside it is a charming hump-backed bridge (fig. 33), now only for pedestrians, which (like those at Rowley's Lock and Broadboyne Bridge) carries an oval stone plaque bearing the name of the lock and its chief engineer, Richard Evans, together with the date, 1792 – a year which must have been alive with activity along this whole stretch, not only with the building of the locks and bridges but with the creation of the banks of the canal itself. The water on the canal was usually a few feet above the level of the Boyne, and stout banks were needed to make sure nothing leaked. They are today a tribute to the thoroughness of Mr Evans and his team, and provide solid ground for going on a quiet and entertaining walk along the Boyne.

The elegance of the bridges and the romance of the old locks – sometimes still accompanied by their rusting machinery – are, despite the occasional intrusion of modern disposables, capable of evoking idyllic times past. We can imagine old vessels being raised or lowered in the locks, with finely dressed nobility looking over the bridge's parapet as the lock-keeper herds the vessel through and sends it on its way up or down the Boyne. The overhanging trees somehow add to the sense of almost magical decay, and bring a lyrical response from anyone who has the good fortune to walk along the path. It was here that, to my delight, I caught one of only two glimpses of a kingfisher I have ever had.

At the start of the walk, near Athlumney, there is a stretch where An Taisce some decades ago revived the sylvan surroundings by planting new trees, which are now well on the way to maturity.

About two and a half kilometres downstream – near Rowley's Lock, on the right-hand bank of the Boyne – there is a lonesome single arch of an ancient bridge known either as Babe's, Rogues' or Robbers' Bridge. James Grace's late-medieval *Annals of Ireland* reported that it was the only bridge not to be devastated by the great flood on the Boyne in 1330 (see page 29). O'Keeffe and Simington's masterly book *Irish Stone Bridges: History and Heritage* (1991) quotes a statute of 1413 to the effect that the bridge was given land to provide money for its own maintenance, though the proceeds were sadly misappropriated by the king's own men in Dublin Castle – perhaps one reason why only a solitary arch today survives out of an original total of about eleven. The documentation just quoted indicates that this small fragment is part of what seems to have been the oldest bridge on the whole of the River Boyne.

The far end of the bridge, on the northern bank of the Boyne, would have continued onto a path which led between the river and Donaghmore (see fig. 101, page 151), one of the oldest religious foundations along the river. That a placename contains the element *Domhnach*, from the Latin *Dominicus* (Sunday), is usually indicative of an early church,

Fig. 34: The sun sets over the ruins of Dunmoe Castle as the gloaming approaches on the banks of the Boyne.

and Domhnach Mór Maige Echnach (as it is called in Irish) is no exception. Aubrey Gwynn and R. Neville Hadcock's *Medieval Religious Houses of Ireland* (1988) says it was built by St Patrick for Cruimthir Cassan (St Cassanus), whose relics were later preserved in the church (which was plundered in 854). The main survivor of the ancient monastery here, its Round Tower, will be discussed later (see page 151), but the National Museum preserves another, much smaller, remnant in the form of a High Cross head which probably, though not certainly, came from Donaghmore. The church with bell-cote still standing on the site is the remnant of a parish church which in its present form, can scarcely be much older than the sixteenth century, though it may well preserve parts of an older church it replaced.

Along the Boyne Walk towards Slane

Below Donaghmore, the Boyne bends eastwards for over a kilometre, providing a charming walk on the south side of the canal. An early-nineteenth-century milestone on a raised platform bears the number '4' and offers a lovely view, closed off at the end by the church of Ardmulchan. But before you reach it there is a further fine castle, on the left or northern bank of the Boyne. This is Dunmoe (fig. 34), about whose history very little is recorded. As with so many castles in the area, the villain Cromwell is supposed to have turned his guns upon it – or at least one, for Wilde recalls that a single cannon ball utilised in his day for balancing a local crane was traditionally said to have been fired by the Lord Protector's army. But Cromwell cannot be blamed for the collapse of that half of this rectangular castle that looks away from the river, as it was still intact in the late eighteenth century, when the castle was occupied and a house was added at the eastern end (fig. 35). A fire of 1799 may have had something to do with its downfall.

Sir William Wilde, one of the few to record any tradition connected with the castle, tells us that it has withstood a number of sieges, the most notable being that of 1641, when a certain Captain Power and a mere handful of men held out in the castle against Irish assailants. Unable to take it, the latter resorted to a stratagem which involved the production of a forged order purporting to have been signed by the Lords Justices Parsons and Borlace in Dublin Castle, at the sight of which Power was induced to surrender.

Some say the castle was built by a de Lacy around 1200, while others maintain it is more likely to date from about the sixteenth century; David Sweetman, in his recent book *The Medieval Castles of Ireland* (2000), opts for a middle date of around the late fourteenth or early fifteenth century, and implies that the castle is something of a cross between a tower-house and a hall-house because it had a tall vaulted hall running the whole of its length on the ground floor. On the slope beside it down to the Boyne is an old ruined church, and beside the riverbank there is a mill, which was operational up until World War I. Stretching right across the river from the mill, a weir provides the reassuring sound of constantly falling water.

Fig. 35: The now-ruined Dunmoe Castle was still entire and lived-in when Gabriel Beranger painted this watercolour of it on visiting the Boyne Valley in 1775. The half of the castle looking away from the river has collapsed in the meantime.

The Boyne Valley

Opposite Dunmoe is Ardmulchan Castle (private), a mansion built by a Scot in the years 1902–4; according to Casey and Rowan's Pevsner-style volume, *North Leinster*, this is 'the Scottish experience in Ireland'. The set of steps leading from the house down to the canal's edge must be one of the longest and most impressive in Ireland.

Farther along, on the south side of the river, is Ardmulchan Church, which, like stout Cortéz, 'silent on a peak in Darien', looks back on the mile-long stretch we have been traversing. The church itself is not inspiring, but it is worth visiting for the view (fig. 36) it provides of one of the most classically beautiful parts of the Boyne, with canal, walk, water, weir, Dunmoe Castle, wooded banks . . . and scarcely a modern development to detract from the vista. This view led Wilde to indulge in one of his more romantic outbursts concerning the Boyne:

> Here the true beauty of the Boyne, its real Rhine-like character, commences. High beetling crags, crowned by feudal halls and ruined chapels – steep, precipitous banks, covered with noblest monarchs of the forest – dells, consecrated to the moonlit dance of sprites and elves, and rock, memorable for their tales of love, and legends of the olden time, catch the eye at

every turn in this noble stream, presenting new beauties, ever-varying pictures, here in sunshine, there in shade, with charming bits of scenery, which simple prose cannot describe: the painter's art alone can embody, or give an accurate representation of these. We 'stop not for brake, and we stay not for stone'; clear and blue the stream runs fast, and we must onwards with its course, skimming lightly over its surface, rather inciting inquiry by our remarks, and directing attention in our researches, than attempting anything like an elaborate or detailed description.

Wilde goes on to tell us that a combined army of Vikings and Leinstermen defeated the high-kingly family of the Southern Uí Néill here in 968; and that this parish church, with its three-storey tower, formerly belonged to the Earl of Kildare, who engaged for it a single priest whose constant duty was to celebrate divine service here. The church bells, according to local tradition, were thrown into the Boyne at Taaffe's Lock, which is just around the corner. The raised location of the church and the Norman motte close to it makes one aware just how deep is the bed that the Boyne has dug itself beneath the plateau of its banks to either side.

Fig. 36: Cloud and sun provide a moody mix above one of the most beautiful stretches of the Boyne where it curves beneath Ardmulchan Church after a long straight stretch past Dunmoe Castle.

Heading towards Slane

In the midst of this entrancing countryside, the Boyne turns northeastwards after Ardmulchan and heads for Broadboyne Bridge (fig. 37), another fine canal bridge by the engineer Richard Evans but here tucked in at the end of the old medieval bridge. Below it is one of the rare instances in the middle reaches of the river where the road follows its twists and turns closely, and provides idyllic views of wooded banks and old mills and weirs. Sir William Wilde again:

> The river here forms a smooth, glass-like sheet of water, and below the bridge affords us one of those striking effects which the weirs upon the Boyne exhibit, a long unbroken line of liquid, bent into a graceful curve, gilded by the sunshine, as it glides in swift but silent track over the long horse-shoe fall, and then breaks into a million streams – its spray dancing in the sunshine, and its bubbles reflecting all the prismatic colours of the rainbow, as it again springs onward in its course.

Fig. 37: An extension at the southern end of Broadboyne Bridge was added in 1792 to allow the tow-path and the canal past it on their way to Slane.

No wonder Wilde went into such raptures over this delightful stretch of river and canal around Stackallan – where, incidentally, the centre of building operations for the Boyne Navigation was located.

Gliding gently onward through the steep and sylvan banks, the river reaches Beauparc. Here is a fine private Palladian mansion built – possibly by the amateur architect Nathaniel Clements – for Gustavus Lambart, a Member of Parliament for Kilbeggan in the neighbouring county of Westmeath. This is a house which uses its location splendidly to see the Boyne – and to be seen from it. In the days when tourist boats came upriver as far as here (see fig. 32, page 53), Beauparc provided a terminus where the visitors disembarked; they then repaired to the nearby railway station to entrain for the journey back to their starting point at Drogheda. Traces of the old train station can be found here, converted into modern houses. The bridge near Stackallan bears the date 1847, being built in that year to provide a speedy link between Navan and Drogheda. Only a little further downstream from Beauparc is a white limestone escarpment known as Maiden Rock or Lover's Leap (fig. 38) – perhaps the Boyne's answer to the Rhine's Lorelei.

Only a short distance downstream (fig. 39, page 62), close to the river, is Carrickdexter Castle, traditionally said to have been built by the Flemings, lords of Slane, and even to have been their stronghold. It was once accompanied by an old family graveyard, but all trace of this has vanished. However, the castle's name makes it much more likely – as Wilde realised – that it was the D'Exeter family, also of Norman origin, who erected it. It is a building of two styles and two stages. Originally there was a four-storey tower-house with vaulted basement, diagonally placed corner towers and small windows. Added to the east was a lower, three-storey extension with a projection on the north face and the remains of some large chimney-pieces that speak of the slightly more relaxed living style of the seventeenth century, which is presumably when this part was built. Visiting the castle, which stands alone in a rather large field, it is lovely to hear the soothing cascade of water going over the

Fig. 38: A watercolour of c. 1800 by James George O'Brien (otherwise known as Oben) shows the Maiden's Rock or Lover's Leap at Fennor, between Beauparc and Slane.

Fig. 39: Below Beauparc, the Boyne curves through a gorge on its way to Carrickdexter and Slane, seen here in the background of this watercolour painted around 1800 by James George O'Brien (or Oben), and now in a private collection.

Fig. 40: The figure of St Peter with his keys on the top of the cross at Baronstown, above Slane, was carved around 1607 to request a prayer for Dame Jennet Dowdall and her second husband, Oliver Plunkett, Lord Baron of Louth, in whose memory she had the cross erected.

weir beneath the building; because of the weir there was a lock here in the eighteenth century. The story is told about this castle (but it is also told about others in the west of Ireland, let it be said) that there was a net in the river which had a line joining it to the castle kitchen so that, should a salmon get caught in the mesh, the cook would be alerted and could immediately go down to collect the fish as the main course for the next meal.

Standing on a hillock overlooking Carrickdexter is an almost four-hundred-year-old limestone cross, Baronstown Cross (fig. 40). Until recently this was on the south side of the road, but the construction of the broadened and straightened highway from Navan to Slane has caused the cross to be on an island between the old and the new roads. The effect is in fact attractive. The outline of the cross, which is over 2 m high, dominates the skyline from a distance. It has a lower shaft supporting a broad, roughly square collar with a much shorter limb above it. All four sides bear inscriptions in Roman lettering, the texts full of contractions and spelling mistakes, asking Saints Peter and Paul to pray for the souls of Oliver Plunkett, Lord Baron of Louth, and his wife Jennet Dowdall.

Plunkett died in 1607 at Tallanstown in County Louth, and there Dame Jennet erected a cross to his memory at Louth Hall; both crosses were probably erected shortly after his death. The names of the two saints invoked are carved near the top of the west and east sides respectively, the same positions on the other two faces being taken up by the Plunkett and Dowdall coats-of-arms.

Slane

From the eminence on which the Baronstown Cross stands, a view can be had of Slane Castle, founded by the Norman family of Fleming in the twelfth century and retained by them until 1641. After various vicissitudes, it finally came into the possession of the Conyngham family, which hailed from Mount Charles in Donegal, in which family the title remains. The present lord of the manor has for over twenty years been running hugely successful rock concerts in the vast field in front of the castle.

What the original castle looked like we do not know, for the building has undergone many changes down the years; but a painting by Thomas Roberts (fig. 41) shows the appearance of this tall square block with its corner turrets before James Wyatt began to transform the structure in 1785 into what we see today. Francis Johnston, the architect who also designed Townley Hall only a few miles farther to the east, took over a good deal of the interior work from 1795, but it was not until thirteen years later that the most unusual room in the castle was built. This is the circular salon or library, which has splendid plasterwork, probably by Thomas Hopper, done in the neo-Gothic style – here making one of its earliest appearances in Ireland. The salon must have been among the rooms shown off with pride by Elizabeth, Marchioness of Conyngham, on the day in 1821 when the castle was visited by King George IV, whose mistress she was. He gave her generous gifts of furniture and other things, some of which were sadly damaged in a major fire in 1991 – although ten years of successful restoration has now brought the castle back to its original glory.

Fig. 41: The fine oil painting by Thomas Roberts, of c. 1773, shows Slane Castle before it was given its present form by the architect James Wyatt in 1785. Now, the Castle offers guided tours at certain times in summer.

Fig. 42: William Burton (later Conyngham), of Slane Castle, whose portrait, painted by the American artist Gilbert Stuart, hangs in the National Gallery in Dublin. He founded the Hibernian Antiquarian Society in 1779 to make the public more aware of the beauties of Ireland's ancient monuments.

The man who got Wyatt and Johnston involved in the alterations to Slane Castle was Colonel William Burton (1733–1796), who adopted the family name Conyngham by royal licence when his uncle, the Earl, died in 1781 and left him the castle and his extensive interests in Donegal. Burton (fig. 42), who lived in the castle before he inherited it, was a Member of Parliament and a Privy Councillor, a teller of the Exchequer, and the first Treasurer of the Royal Irish Academy, among other things. In 1779 he founded the Hibernian Antiquarian Society with the laudable aim of trying to make the world aware of the beauties of Ireland's ancient buildings. At Slane one of his guests was the famous architect James Gandon, whom he encouraged in his plans to build Dublin's Custom House; the two men later fell out because Gandon failed to consult Burton Conyngham about the Four Courts. Gabriel Beranger, a Dutch watercolourist who spent most of his life in Dublin, was another invited to stay, and on the day of one of his visits, in the summer of 1779, strange early medieval objects known as latchets were unearthed in the grounds of the castle. (We are fortunate that Beranger has left us a number of watercolours of castles and abbeys along the Boyne which help us re-create the surroundings of the river above and below Slane as they looked in the later eighteenth century.)

In 1797, the year after Burton Conyngham died, his nephew, the first Marquess Conyngham (husband of George IV's mistress, mentioned above), employed Francis Johnston to add a tall belfry to the Church of Ireland church that had been built in the village of Slane much earlier in the century and, like its Catholic counterpart, dedicated to the National Apostle, St Patrick. The church's most interesting features – the monuments let into the exterior walls at the western end – had nothing to do with Slane originally; most of them were brought here from St Collan's Church in Stackallan when that church was demolished over forty years ago. The centrepiece is a late-medieval doorway, with a single, effectively-carved head on top. To its left is a wedge-shaped tombstone with cross and sword, dated *c.* 1300 and commemorating Sir Richard Dexter. Apart from the first two Latin words of the inscription, 'pater noster', the remainder – asking for charity for the soul of Sir Richard – were written in Norman French but in mirror image, suggesting that the mason may have been illiterate and was copying the inscription from the wrong side of his paper model. This slab is balanced on the other side of the doorway by another of similar shape, decorated with a cross and floral motifs.

One of the most elaborate carvings in the whole Boyne Valley is the Barnewall coat-of-arms above the doorway (fig. 43). Each individual feature stands out in high relief, making the tablet something of a sculptural *tour-de-force*. The arms, which are of the Barnewalls of Crickstown – a branch of a family who owned extensive lands down as far as north Dublin – consist of a shield with ermine decoration, above which is a helmet, the whole capped by a falcon sitting on its nest and flanked by luxurious foliage. The Latin inscription beneath tells us that this is the shield, or escutcheon, of Barnaby Barnewall, Second Justice of the King's Chief Bench, and that his wife was Margaret Plunkett.

Around the corner, on the southern side of the church vestry, is the headless effigy of an ecclesiastic on a wedge-shaped slab with pointed foot. He is dressed in an alb, has his hands folded across his body, and is carved in such an assured and dignified manner that John Hunt, in his great book *Irish Medieval Figure Sculpture, 1200–1600: Study of Irish Tombs with Notes on Costume and Armour* (1974), was inclined to ascribe it to a late-twelfth- or early-thirteenth-century workshop located in the West of England or in Dublin. He linked it to the effigy thought to be that of Simon de Rochfort in the Church of Saints Peter and Paul in Newtown Trim (see page 167), but the original presence of the effigy at Painestown – whence it was brought four kilometres northwards to Slane – has yet to be satisfactorily explained. Hunt listed this effigy as the oldest known example in Ireland – even earlier, he thought, than that of Simon de Rochfort. The intriguing question remains as to which ecclesiastical figure living in the Painestown area around the year 1200 felt himself sufficiently important to have an effigy made to be placed over his tomb. Where Painestown led, the country obviously followed, and the Middle Ages in Ireland saw the creation of many other effigies of ecclesiastics, including one in the grounds of Slane Castle which was carved about two hundred years later and which, according to C. E. F. Trench, William Burton Conyngham helped save 'from the depredations of the soldiers' in the cavalry barracks in Navan.

In rescuing this episcopal effigy from destruction, Conyngham was assisted by Slane's most famous rector, Mervyn Archdall (1723–1791), who is commemorated on a recumbent slab in the church grounds. He was a founder-member of Burton Conyngham's Hibernian

Fig. 43: The late-fifteenth-century Barnewall coat-of-arms stands out in high relief above the west doorway of the Protestant church in Slane, and can be counted as one of the most intricate carvings anywhere in the Boyne Valley.

Antiquarian Society in 1779, and his enthusiasm came to the fore in his most famous work, *Monasticon Hibernicum, or An History of the Abbies, Priories and Other Religious Houses of Ireland*, published in Dublin in 1786.

Just over the wall from where Archdall lies buried is the likely site of a very early religious foundation, St Erc's Hermitage (fig. 44), which is in the private grounds of Slane Castle. St Erc who, according to *The Annals of Ulster*, died in 513, is thought to have been an associate of St Patrick; the ninth-century *Tripartite Life of St Patrick* portrays him as the only follower of the pagan King Lóegaire of Tara who rose to greet St Patrick when the latter came to confront the king's druids. The Middle Irish tale *The Battle of Dún na nGedh* – whose veracity obviously has to be taken with several grains of salt – tells of how St Erc used to stand up to his armpits in the Boyne singing his psalms, with the book laid on the bank. He lived on three sprigs of cress and a goose egg and a half *per diem*, and uttered a curse on the day of a great feast when someone took his egg and a half away. While the building known as St Erc's Hermitage preserves his name, it was not built until around a thousand years after his death.

Slane was probably a monastic establishment by the eighth century, and very possibly before. Archdall mentions the tradition that Dagobert, Prince of Austrasia (650–679), was spirited away as a child from his home on the European continent because his life was in danger, and was brought to Slane for his schooling, before being returned to France to become King of Austrasia; he is related to the subject of the well-known French song *Le bon roi Dagobert*. The monastery had Ireland's oldest known Round Tower, which has long since disappeared without trace but which is known to have been burned by the Vikings in 948, along with St Erc's crozier, Celechair – the monastery's reader – and 'a bell the best of all bells'. Indeed, the monastery must have been a prosperous one, for the Irish, the Vikings and the Normans took turns attacking it over the next few hundred years; only after the

Fig. 44: George Petrie's atmospheric engraving (c. 1820) of the attractive late medieval church known as St Erc's Hermitage, now in the private grounds of Slane Castle.

Fleming family began to build a castle here in the later 1170s (perhaps the Norman motte on top of the hill?) was its bishopric merged with others to become the single bishopric of Meath – thanks, doubtless, to Simon de Rochfort, whom we have already met at Clonard (see page 25) and will encounter again at Newtown Trim (see page 165). Pilgrims must have come to Slane during the Middle Ages to venerate the relics of some no longer identifiable saint for, up on top of the Hill of Slane, within the walled area of the medieval church, there are two large triangular stones that would have formed the gables of a house-shaped reliquary of a kind better known from the western half of the country. The late-medieval Lebor Breac tells of 260 persons who came from the east on pilgrimage and died in Slane on one day, and who were buried in the cemetery there.

From this cemetery there is a wonderful panorama stretching north, south and east, giving vistas across many counties. The Hill of Slane is also traditionally the location where St Patrick started his battle of wits with King Lóegaire of Tara and his druids by lighting the first Paschal Fire in Ireland in the year 433, although – as George Eogan has suggested – the literary sources would make the great Passage Grave cemetery of Brú na Bóinne just as likely a place for the saint to have kindled his Easter fire. The buildings we see crowning the hilltop today were almost certainly not built by the time the Scottish King Robert Bruce passed through Slane in 1315, dating more likely from the early sixteenth century. In 1512, Christopher Fleming, Baron of Slane, and his wife Elizabeth Stuckly granted St Erc's Hermitage to Father Malachy O'Bryan and Brother Donagh O'Bryen, two Franciscans whom Fleming then moved up the hill to the new Franciscan friary which he had founded there. At the Dissolution of the Monasteries in 1540 its 'church and belfry, dormitory, garden and two closes' were seized by the Crown; they were granted to Sir James Fleming three years later for the large fee of one penny. For all that, the Flemings were good to the Catholic clergy, and one of them, the 'titular' Bishop of Cashel, was entertained to dinner by them – although he was secretly betrayed by another guest and brought to Dublin to be hanged.

The main feature of the friary is the tall tower standing at its western end (see fig. 91, page 135), in contrast to the usual Franciscan practice of placing the tower closer to the middle of the church. Perhaps the variation from the norm was permitted because this was a house not of the First Order of Franciscans but of the Third, which allowed married people to be members of the congregation and which involved itself in pastoral work and teaching. One manuscript of a biblical concordance, though written probably in Dorchester, is known to have been used in this Third Order foundation in Slane.

Side by side with it, Christopher Fleming founded in the same year a secular college for four priests, four clerics and four choristers. With the benefit of 100 acres of land granted to them, the dozen must have lived well, as evidenced by the comparative opulence of the buildings that still survive, with large fireplaces to keep them warm on winter evenings. A cloister garth at the centre is surrounded on three sides, the main frontage being to the south, where the somewhat abraded arms of France and England are inserted above the doorway. The windows are well decorated. Two carved heads can be seen farther to the left.

It is because the church on the hill was regarded as being 'of difficult ascent' that the Protestant church, built in 1738, was set farther down the slope and nearer to the river. Just to the east of it grew up what C. E. F. ('Terry') Trench describes as 'one of the most attractive villages in Ireland' in his valuable little book, *Slane: Slane Town Trail, Newgrange* (1976), the latest edition of which appeared in 1995. The village may well have developed on the

Fig. 45: The broad bridge of Slane offers the Boyne a wide choice of arches to flow under after its waters tumble gently over a weir farther to the left.

site of the 'Green of Slane', the cross on which – according to the old *Irish Nennius* – was taken up into the air and its fragments dispersed to Tailten, Tara and Fennor. Precisely when this curious event is meant to have happened is not recorded, but history may possibly have come full circle, because the remains of a small High Cross discovered just over a decade ago at Fennor, on the opposite side of the Boyne (see below), have been brought to Slane for display beside the altar in the Catholic church above the centre of the village.

This latter church has attached to it a particularly touching story, related by Dean Cogan, the historian of the diocese of Meath, whose memorial – with bust – can be found in the north transept. The church was built by Father Michael O'Hanlon, who was born near Dowth, graduated in Bordeaux and who was staying in the Irish College in Paris when he heard a voice asking if anyone knew of a Colonel Conyngham from Ireland who was, at the time, arraigned before a Revolutionary Tribunal. Father O'Hanlon agreed to go to the Tribunal, where he gave a very good character reference for his fellow Meath man, Henry Conyngham, whereupon the colonel's life was spared. Sometime after Conyngham had duly succeeded to Slane Castle on the death of his uncle William Burton, in 1796, Father O'Hanlon returned to his native county and, on arrival, he went along to the castle to congratulate the new owner. He was heartily thanked for his life-saving speech, and was asked what wish he would like granted. When he said that his parishioners had only a barn for worship, and a rather tumble-down one at that, Conyngham gave him the site for a new church and helped him to build it too – along with a belfry in the form of a Round Tower, which could be taken as a symbolic renewal of the one destroyed by the 'Danes' eight hundred and fifty years earlier.

The village has a beautifully symmetrical arrangement of four houses which, as it were, cut off the corners of a square to make an octagon out of what is today nevertheless called The Square. All four houses are identical except for their doors. The first was built in 1767. Local stories of their origins differ. Some say they were built for four Conyngham sisters who did not speak with one another, others that they were erected for the priest, the doctor, the magistrate and the police. Given that there is no record of a quartet of Conyngham sisters, one suspects the true explanation may have been more prosaic than either tradition.

Slane, which is proud of its little local hotel, has become an important – but also a dangerous – crossroads on the Drogheda–Navan and Dublin–Derry routes. Even more perilous is the great slope heading downwards from the village towards the Boyne Bridge (fig. 45), where many a lorry brake has failed and far too many lives have been lost in consequence. Halfway down the hill on the right is the original but now disused gate to Slane Castle (fig. 46), a rather massive turreted affair designed in the first years of the nineteenth century by Francis Johnston, the architect who helped with the interior work for the castle from 1795 onwards. Over the gate is the fine coat-of-arms of Henry Conyngham (the man whose life Father O'Hanlon helped save) and his wife Elizabeth Denison, displaying the earl's coronet bestowed upon Henry in 1797. Beneath this is a badge of the Illustrious Order of St Patrick, a now defunct institution set up by George III to encourage loyalty among the Irish peers; it had twenty-two Knights Companions along with a Grand Master, plus the sovereign himself. The badge was to draw attention to Conyngham having been made one of the Knights Companions in 1801. The order was to benefit from Lady Elizabeth Conyngham's being the mistress of George IV; as noted, he came to visit her in Slane Castle in 1821. George gave her jewellery that had been worn by his queen, Charlotte, but on his death Lady Conyngham decided to return it all to Dublin Castle. There the decision was made to rework the jewels into insignia for the Illustrious Order of St Patrick, which apparently did not have any, and so came into being an eight-pointed star of Brazilian diamonds with an emerald shamrock and ruby cross at its centre, as well as a badge with rubies, diamonds and a gold harp and crown. In time, these valuables came to

Fig. 46: The now disused early-nineteenth-century gate of Slane Castle stands beside the road that rises steeply upwards from the Boyne Bridge at Slane. Its architect was Francis Johnston.

be regarded as the Irish Crown Jewels. They achieved fame in 1907 when they were stolen from Dublin Castle only a few days before a visit by George's descendant, Edward VII. Their disappearance remains clouded in mystery, and the search for them still continues without a clue.

Let into a wall at the bottom of the hill is a copy of a plaque (see fig. 48, page 72) designed by the great Cork sculptor Seamus Murphy, R.H.A., to commemorate Slane's equally great poet, Francis Ledwidge (fig. 47), who was killed fighting near Ypres during World War I on 31 July 1917. Ledwidge's talent was first discovered by a local curate, Father Edward Smyth, and later fostered by Lord Dunsany, as we saw on page 44. On the poet's death Dunsany wrote a glowing obituary in *The Irish Times* (as reprinted in *The Irish Book Lover*, November–December 1917):

If mere words may be an offering to the dead, I offer these in place of wreath or flowers to the memory of Francis Ledwidge. On July 31st, this rare poet, a lance-corporal with the Enniskillen Fusiliers, was killed in action by a shell. He was born in 1891 in a peasant's cottage in Slane, lived nearly all his life there, and has crystallised his love for it in many verses that will far outlive the length of his own brief years. In 1912 he first brought me some of his poems, which astonished me by their freshness and their beauty, as they do to this day. Nobody seems to have cared for them among the few that had seen them around his native village, or, perhaps, they only read them to laugh at the faults which were to be found in those days; and so my admiration for his genius seems to have been the first encouragement that he had. How this can have been it is hard to understand, for here are lines that show not promise merely, but the actual presence of genius, full grown, with its wings spread, written when he was only sixteen:

Fig. 47: Francis Ledwidge, the Boyne's most talented poet, could have earned international recognition in his day had not World War I cut short his all-too-brief life in 1917.

> *And wondrous impudently sweet,*
> *Half of him passion, half conceit,*
> *The blackbird calls adown the street*
> *Like the piper of Hamelin.*

Has anything finer been said of the blackbird in all English literature?

From that time he began seriously to write poetry, or happily rather, merrily and easily, and soon his first book was finished, *Songs of the Fields*. It was as though he had discovered some golden box, out of which, whenever he wished, he took a poem from the works of some unknown master that filled the box, for he brought me poems quicker than you would think he could write them, and finer than you would dream a peasant could make.

He nearly always wrote of the fields and lanes of his own beloved home, and even when in Serbia or Salonica, Gallipoli, Egypt, France, or Belgium, up to the end some happy inspiration guided homeward his dreams, so that even in those far lands, even at war, he wrote of his wild birds and wild roses, and equally wayward loves, as truly as when leaning out at evening to watch the chaffinches from the window he loved.

Roses will bloom in lanes in Meath for thousands of years to come, and blackbirds will charm other hearts, and the Boyne still sweep to the sea, and others may love these things as Ledwidge loved them, but they were all so much pictured upon his heart, and he sang so gladly of them, that something is lost which those fields would have given up, and may never give again . . .

All through the war he wrote whenever he had leisure: some of these poems are collected in his book, *Songs of Peace*, as many more are yet in manuscript. All his poems he used to bring or send me, and the best of them all I received the day he died: it tells how his dead love came to him out of a 'fairy place', so that he knew his end was come:

> *On the edge of life I seemed to hover,*
> *For I knew my love had come at last;*
> *That my joy was past and my gladness over.*

I never wished to handicap him by exaggerated praise, but now that no mistake of mine can hurt him, if mistake it be, I give my opinion that, if Ledwidge had lived, this lover of all seasons in which the blackbird sings would have surpassed even Burns, and Ireland would have lawfully claimed, as she may do even yet, the greatest of peasant singers.

Much play was made of the peer discovering the peasant poet, but such comment does no justice to the genius of Ledwidge, who, though a great supporter of those who died for Ireland in 1916, was still prepared to join the British army and fight 'an enemy common to our civilisation' in World War I. His regard for Thomas McDonagh, and his revulsion and deep sadness at McDonagh's execution after the 1916 rising, led to the writing of one of Ledwidge's most famous poems, which could equally serve as an epitaph for the poet himself, who lies buried in a foreign grave:

> *He shall not hear the bittern cry*
> *In the wild sky where he is lain,*
> *Nor voices of the sweeter birds*
> *Above the wailing of the rain.*

Nor shall he know when loud March blows
Thro' snows her fanfare shrill,
Blowing to flame the golden cup
Of many an upset daffodil.

But when the Dark Cow leaves the moor,
And pastures with greedy weeds,
Perhaps he'll hear her low at morn
Lifting her horn in pleasant meads.

Ledwidge's was a truly lyrical voice, that of a love poet whose songs are tinged at times with sadness but whose feeling for melody and music rank him among the finest and most feeling of modern Irish poets.

The peasant's cottage where he grew up overlooks the Boyne almost a kilometre from Slane on the Drogheda road and here the original Seamus Murphy plaque (fig. 48) is let into the wall beside the entrance. The house, now an attractive museum in Ledwidge's memory, run by a Trust and tended by his many local admirers, is open virtually all the year round. A poem entitled 'The Home of my Wish' expresses Ledwidge's own feelings towards this house where he grew to maturity:

Thro' my garden set among the trees
The wild convolvulus might steal,
And honey bells for pedlar bees
With silence to the silence peal.
I would have all things fair and wild,
Nor seek account of slip, or seed,
But straying like a woodland child
Where lovely wantonness might lead.

And near my house among the leaves
A river from the hills should sing,
And swallows from my sheltered eaves
Should set the ivy fluttering.
Thro' secret ways of shine and shade
At night my love should come to me,
A comely and a joyous maid,
Pure as the morning's purity.

Fig. 48: The plaque by the Cork sculptor Seamus Murphy commemorating Francis Ledwidge is let into the wall of the poet's cottage east of Slane that is now a museum to his memory. A copy of the plaque is inserted into a wall beside the Boyne Bridge at Slane.

He weaves magic with his lilting words, and has a tremendous rapport with nature, one much to be envied by us modern suburbanites. He creates wonderment in using lovely botanical names such as 'convolvulus' and 'eglantine', and through the gentle evocation of the haunting blackbird's song in the poem so highly praised by Lord Dunsany. Liam O'Meara tells in *A Lantern on the Wave: A Study of the Life of the Poet Francis Ledwidge* (1999) how the poet went to work in a grocery shop in the Dublin suburb of Rathfarnham but became so nostalgic for Slane that he woke up one night and wrote 'Behind the Closed Eye', which provided the verse cited by Dunsany. The preceding stanza should also be

quoted here, as it is Ledwidge's best evocation of the village, with the Catholic church and the belfry that he dreamed of when in Dublin or far away on Flanders Field:

> *Above me smokes the little town,*
> *With its whitewashed walls and roofs of brown*
> *And its octagon spire toned smoothly down*
> *As the holy minds within.*

Fig. 49: The weir at Slane where water is diverted under the bridge to serve Jebb's Mill (seen in the background) which was one of the most progressive in the country when its wheels started turning in 1766.

He was a premature loss not only for Ireland and the Boyne but for the world.

Just beside the plaque to Ledwidge at Slane Bridge is the entrance to Jebb's Mill (fig. 49), which was served by a mill-race that went under the northernmost arch of the bridge. Arthur Young, who toured Ireland in 1776, thought the mill superior to anything he had seen in England, and General Charles Vallancey, later to be the King's Chief Engineer in Ireland, said it was built 'with so much undecorated elegance as renders the whole light and pleasing to the eye', showing that even industrial buildings could benefit from the graceful architectural style of the eighteenth century.

It was opened in 1766, with Blayney Townley Balfour of Townley Hall as the main shareholder; others included Colonel William Burton, whom we have already encountered, and his usually absentee brother, Lord Conyngham, whose castle Burton looked after long before he became its owner in 1781. The builder of the mill, and the man who gave his name to it, was David Jebb, the Engineer, Secretary and Treasurer of the Boyne Navigation, whose operations he influenced in the interest of the Slane mill (see page 53). It was the largest mill in the Ireland of its day, and the tall mill building is still an impressive sight. In over two centuries of activity, and under a considerable variety of owners, it produced flour, linen, cotton and rayon among other things until its doors were finally forced to close in 1994.

David Jebb was presumably the builder and occupier of the Georgian millhouse, which later functioned as the Boyneville Hotel, serving lunches to the passengers who took the tourist steamer upriver from Oldbridge between 1903 and 1914; one hopes it will revert to that role under its new owners, who have great plans for this important old industrial complex.

Those tourist trips were the brainchild of James McCann, the Drogheda miller who tried to breathe new life into the Boyne Navigation in the early decades of the last century, and about whom Standish O'Grady wrote the lovely little bit of doggerel quoted in C.E.F. Trench's handsome volume on Slane:

> By the Boyne and the Blackwater I sat down and wept
> When I thought of the centuries Erin had slept.
> By the Boyne and the Blackwater I lept up and sang,
> When I thought of the canal boats and Jamesy McCann.

The mill looks across the Boyne at Fennor, home of an unnamed singer recalled by Ledwidge:

> Sweetest voice of vale and hill,
> Kneaded with thine own today – my soul with rapture fill!
> Ethereal maid of Fennor plain
> Yearn I to hear, to hear thee sing again.

On the north-facing hill sloping down to the Boyne is an early-seventeenth-century house incorporating the remains of an earlier tower-house. It is three storeys high with gable chimney-stacks and a series of large gaunt windows, but little is known about its history. The same is true of the church beneath it, whence came the High Cross that is now in the Catholic church in Slane (see page 68).

At the foot of the slope, the canal passes by the Boyne's edge. Its independent course had stopped on the northern bank at Carrickdexter and then by-passed the weir beneath Slane Castle before taking up again at the lock just upstream from the 13-arch medieval bridge that crosses the river beside Jebb's Mill. After going under an extra arch on the south side of the bridge, the canal continues past Fennor to Rossnaree (also spelled Rosnaree), where it passes through a lock and under another bridge before merging again with the river for a short time.

The Bend of the Boyne, Brú na Bóinne and Duleek

This is where the Bend of the Boyne, the river's most famous stretch, finally begins. We saw on page 19 how the Boyne's early progress makes a large curve over the river's first ten miles (16 km) or so, but the bend here is something different: the river does not go through flat countryside, as it does near its source. In this part of its course the Boyne made a bed for itself a mere 12,000 years ago when, after the glaciers had retreated at the end of the last Ice Age, the river had to find an outlet to the sea. Coming from the west, it found its way blocked straight ahead by a long ridge of carboniferous shales with a light covering of glacial till, upon which the three great mounds of Knowth, Dowth and, at a slightly lower level, Newgrange were to be built. Consequently the river turned southwards, running parallel to the ridge, then headed northeastwards through something of a gorge before emerging into more level countryside near Oldbridge, where it is joined by the Mattock River.

Obviously, the fertile if ill-drained podsolic soil of this island of rocks encouraged the Neolithic farmers to start clearing the forests – oak and elm on the high ground, hazel, birch and alder on the valley floor – before sowing their crops and building their great tombs (discussed on pages 100–23). As they did so, during fifteen hundred years of the Late Stone and Early Bronze Ages – from, say, 3300 BC to 1800 BC – they created a landscape which came to be revered over time and which gives the impression of having a sacred aura.

The most dominant monuments in the area are the three great Passage Graves of Newgrange (fig. 50), Knowth and Dowth, the first two certainly and the last quite probably being once surrounded by smaller satellite tombs. If we were paddling along the river and going with the current, the first of the great tombs we would meet is Knowth, then Newgrange, and finally Dowth. New ritual activity of a kind that escapes our ken surrounded the great mounds in the second half of the third millennium BC. This took the

Fig. 50: The white quartz coating of the Newgrange façade makes itself felt when seen from the low-lying trees on the opposite bank of the river.

Fig. 51: Roman gold coin pendants once deposited at Newgrange, and now in the National Museum, demonstrate how the great Passage Tomb must still have been a sacred place in the fourth century AD, with a magnetism attracting devotees from far and wide.

form of creating round enclosures made of earth and stone combined, or wooden versions of Stonehenge, some with curious pits containing votive offerings of animals. It was probably in one of the centuries around 2000 BC that great chunky stones (see fig. 84, page 122) were set up in an irregular circle around Newgrange. Some of the smaller ritual sites lie not far from the Boyne; one, although it is really only visible from the air, is located near the weir south of Newgrange. Close by, in the plain only just above the level of the river and on land most suitable for pastoral activity, are isolated Passage Graves, as yet unexcavated, but clearly visible from the main mound. In a field some distance to the east of Dowth there is also an important round enclosure, so much larger than normal ring-forts that it probably has nothing to do with them or the medieval period, but is ascribable rather to this flurry of sacral activity in the Bend of the Boyne in the third and second millennia BC.

The old ford which crosses the Boyne in this area is at Rossnaree, where the river begins to turn eastwards to run parallel with the shaly ridge. Here the ancient midland way, the *Slighe Midluachra*, traversed the Boyne, en route from Tara towards Ulster. It is also here that we begin to appreciate not only the reverence which the ancients of the Iron Age – the centuries on either side of Christ's lifetime – presumably had for Newgrange, but also how Rossnaree came to play an important role as both a ford and a royal palace. This we learn from the story of the burial of the legendary King Cormac mac Airt, who died at his house at Cletty, which may have occupied the site today marked by the attractive Rossnaree House, a commanding position that would have given a splendid view across the river to the great tombs.

Cormac asked his people not to bury him in the *Brú* (i.e., Newgrange) because, being a 'proto-Christian' king, he did not share the pagan beliefs of those buried within the great mound. He wanted to be buried at Rossnaree, with his face to the rising sun. On his death, his servants deliberated carefully but decided after all to bring him to the Brú, for that was where his predecessors as Kings of Tara had been buried. Three times the men who carried his remains tried to cross the Boyne, but three times its waters welled up to impede them. Taking this seemingly supernatural hint, they finally agreed to respect the old man's wishes and buried him at Rossnaree. But where his grave is no one knows.

The reason why Cormac lived at Rossnaree and not in the royal residence at Tara was that the loss of one of his eyes made him no longer fit to be a king, 'for it was not lawful that a king with a personal blemish should reside at Tara'. His death is said to have come about because he choked on a salmon bone.

This fish, once abundant in the Boyne, also plays a role in the story of how Cormac's contemporary, the legendary Fionn mac Cumhaill, acquired his wisdom quite by chance on the banks of the river. A certain druid, Finnéigeas by name, had been waiting for years by the water to capture the Salmon of Knowledge in the river, and he finally succeeded in doing so. However, just as he was cooking it, the bold Finn came along and, by accident, burned his thumb on the salmon. He put his finger in his mouth to soothe the pain, and thereby inherited the power of divination from the fish before the poor, patient druid could!

It might also have been the prospect of Boyne salmon that attracted the Roman-era visitors who came here and deposited the gold coin-pendants that have been found around Newgrange (fig. 51).

Perhaps because of its old pagan associations, the Bend of the Boyne seems to have kept large early Christian religious foundations at arm's length. The nearest other than Slane is Duleek, five kilometres to the southeast.

Duleek was founded on the Nanny River sometime before 489 by St Cianán, who had been given the Gospel by St Patrick; he is said to have built here the first stone church in Ireland. No one knows how old the simple stone church in Duleek is, but John Bradley has argued that it was dedicated not to St Cianán but rather to St Patrick. Yet, even if the church was not erected until long after the deaths of both saints, it is clear that Duleek was an important monastery in the ninth and tenth centuries. This can be deduced from the existence here of a small High Cross of the period (see figs. 93 and 94, pages 139–40). It bears some enigmatic scenes, but the quality of its carving is on a par with that from Monasterboice (see pages 83 and 142) and Kells, two other major monastic foundations on the Boyne Valley's periphery. There is also the head of a second cross (fig. 52) here which, though incomplete, helps to emphasise the importance of the foundation in the last centuries of the first millennium.

Scarcely much later must have been the Round Tower, up against which the existing later medieval square tower was built. The latter proved to be the more permanent and better constructed, for the Round Tower collapsed at some period unknown, so that all we have left of it now is its negative impression in the north side of the surviving square tower. The tower and its accompanying church presumably belonged to the Augustinian monastery at Duleek, which must have had an earlier church there, of which a Romanesque head-capital of the twelfth century was the only obvious survivor, before the present ruined structure was erected.

In the later medieval nave-and-chancel church there are some interesting grave monuments, including a late-fifteenth-century Preston tomb that has no effigy but does have tomb-surrounds carved with a representation of the crucified Christ and figures of St Catherine, the Archangel Michael and, it is supposed, Thomas of Canterbury. Another plainer example was erected to the memory of John Bellewe, who 'was shot in the belly in Oughrim fight the first of July 1691'. Even more curious is the grandiose effigy of the Meath bishop Dr Cusack, who died three years earlier – 'a man of great merit for his learning and prudence and earnestness', according to his contemporary, St Oliver Plunkett. One side of the tomb slab bears the effigy, the other the rough-out for it. The latter is the better preserved, because it lay face-down for so long before being placed upright in such a way that both sides of the slab could be seen. The work is the product of a school of carvers,

Fig. 52: The head of a ninth-century High Cross stands on what may have been its original base in the medieval church at Duleek. On its face it bears a carving of the crucified Christ.

active in County Meath in the later seventeenth century, which was probably also responsible for other quaint effigies farther north in the county.

The important early-seventeenth-century crosses in Duleek are discussed on pages 177–8.

Let us return once more to where

> *The skylark's flight is curled*
> *O'er the vale o' Rosnaree*

in the words of Francis Ledwidge, where he would

> *Give an eye for a moment's peep*
> *At the vale o' Rosnaree*
> *Where Boyne waves half reluctant creep*
> *Athwart their Mother sea.*

The influence of the Cistercians who came to Mellifont (see page 153) in 1142 can be seen in the place names hereabouts, particularly in the suffix grange, meaning an outfarm. 'Newgrange' is one such place name. Among the many brilliant maps in Geraldine Stout's very valuable contribution to *Atlas of the Irish Rural Landscape: Past, Present, Future* (1997), edited by F. H. A. Aalen and Kevin Whelan, is one that shows just how much land the Cistercians once owned in the Bend of the Boyne. They would have worked it themselves, being usually acknowledged as the introducers of organised agriculture to this country. It was the Cistercians who built the original mill at Breo, although only traces of the mill-race survive to the present day. Breo is, interestingly, the only still extant placename to recall the old name for the Bend of the Boyne – Brú na Bóinne.

Near the mill, the Boyne Canal once more changes banks for a short while, cutting off the southwestern curve of the river to avoid some of the small islands which, lurking here, make navigation difficult. Below Newgrange the canal returns to the south side once again. There is a lock at Staleen Upper and another, after almost five kilometres, at Staleen Lower.

Along here is the Boyne's second-newest bridge (the newest being that just completed for the Dublin–Belfast motorway a few miles above Drogheda), built to take pedestrian traffic from the new Brú na Bóinne Interpretative Centre to Knowth and Newgrange. Gone are the days when the public could roll up to the Passage Graves and go straight to the tumuli from the car park. In the hope of minimising damage to the monuments through controlling the ever-increasing traffic – and, indeed, in the hope that it might actually decrease – Dúchas, the heritage service, built this new reception centre not far from Donore where tourists can buy tickets (groups and coach-tours have to book many months in advance) before being transported by minibus to the site of their choice. Inside the Centre is a partial reconstruction of the chamber at Newgrange, re-creating the effect of the penetration of the sun's rays into the tomb at the midwinter solstice, in order to give some idea of what the reality is like to those who are unable or unwilling to go into the chamber itself. A restaurant, toilets and an exhibition with models, as well as a bookshop, are among the other facilities provided in this pleasant gateway to the magical world of Brú na Bóinne.

We should not pass by Dowth without remembering the Fenian, poet and journalist John Boyle O'Reilly (1844–1890), who was born here, son of a schoolmaster at the Netterville Institute for orphaned children. He was condemned to death in 1866 for being

Fig. 53: The memorial with marble bust in the old church at Netterville, near Dowth, was erected to honour John Boyle O'Reilly, a Fenian who escaped captivity in Australia to become the renowned editor of the Boston Pilot.

a member of the Irish Republican Brotherhood, but the sentence was commuted to penal servitude in Australia. From there he escaped by whaler and headed, via Liverpool, to Boston, where in the 1870s he became editor of the newspaper *The Boston Pilot*. In Boston he campaigned against anti-Semitism and colour prejudice. He always hankered after his birthplace, although he knew the British Government would never permit him to return. He was visited in Boston by an Augustinian priest from Drogheda, a Father Anderson, to whom he subsequently wrote a letter of nostalgia:

> I may never return to Drogheda, but I send my love to the very fields and trees along the Boyne from Drogheda to Slane. Some time, for my sake, go out to Dowth, alone, and go up on the moat, and look across the Boyne, over to Rossnaree to the Hill of Tara, and turn eyes all round from Tara to New Grange and Knowth and Slane and Mellifont and Oldbridge and you will see there the pictures that I carry forever in my brain and heart – vivid as the last day I looked on them. If you go into the old church yard at Dowth, you will find my initials cut on a stone on the wall of the old church. I should like to be buried just under that spot, and, please God, perhaps I may be.

The church he refers to is a late-medieval church that once served the parishioners of the small settlement which had originally used the great Passage Grave as a fortified motte.

On his death, O'Reilly was buried in the large Holyhood cemetery in Brookline, Massachusetts, just outside Boston. As Moira Corcoran was able to establish, permission was finally granted in 1893 to have the stone with O'Reilly's initials removed from the small church in Dowth and sent – or brought – to Brookline to be inserted into his rather monumental tombstone. His wish to be buried under the stone which he had inscribed was thus finally granted, although there is no sign of the stone on his tomb today. According to Henry Boylan's lovely book *The Boyne: A Valley of Kings* (1988), the stone was removed from Dowth only around the middle of the last century when O'Reilly's American admirers came here to erect a memorial in his honour (fig. 53), equipped with Irish and American flags, mottoes and symbols, swords and shamrocks, stars and stripes – and a white marble bust of the great patriot, poet and journalist himself.

Fig. 54: The remarkable staircase and dome at the centre of Townley Hall, the masterpiece that the architect Francis Johnston built around 1798.

Oldbridge, Mellifont and the Battle of the Boyne

Near where the Boyne reaches its most northerly point before the estuary, it is joined by the Mattock River, close to where the road from Dowth to Drogheda meets that coming from Slane. The Boyne forms a great curve before the confluence, near which is the entrance to Townley Hall, home of a robin recalled by Francis Ledwidge:

In joyous youth long, long ago
Beside the river Boyne,
Through lonely woods and sparkling streams
I've wandered many a time.
I love to scan those distant days
And sadly I recall
Each hour I sat near the red-breast bird
That piped in Townley Hall.

The house (fig. 54) was designed by Francis Johnston, whose work we have already encountered in Slane (see pages 63 and 69), and built in the 1790s by Blayney Townley Balfour, whom we have also met (see page 74) as the main shareholder of Jebb's Mill at Slane. Now a school, it was in recent times home to the late, great geologist and polymath Frank Mitchell (1912–1997), who did so much to bridge the gap between the sciences and the humanities in Ireland during the second half of the twentieth century, and who encouraged George Eogan to undertake his first excavation of a Passage Grave in the grounds, close to the Slane–Drogheda road. Not far away, and adjoining the Mattock at Monknewtown, is a henge monument excavated by David Sweetman, with close by it a fine mid-nineteenth-century mill (fig. 55), which did not in fact remain active for long, as a reduction in the amount of grain available caused it to be offered for sale in the Incumbered Estates Court in 1856. Higher up the Mattock was another large mill, at Mellifont, which has been demolished. The same fate befell much of the old Cistercian monastery beside it – it was raided for building stones in the eighteenth century – but enough of it fortunately remains for us to appreciate Mellifont as one of the great treasures of the Boyne Valley, savoured as much for its peace and quiet as for the quality of the masonry it once had, which will be discussed in greater detail on page 153.

The Boyne makes a habit of changing its course when joined by a tributary, and the confluence with the Mattock is no exception. The major river succeeds in making almost a half-circle, first northwards and then eastwards, making its first contact with County Louth – its last great curve before it reaches Drogheda. The canal outstrips the river, making a shorter curve around Oldbridge House, a rather dull structure on the south side of the river dating from the eighteenth and nineteenth centuries. The canal finally comes to an end at the Oldbridge Lower Lock, below which the boats were able to navigate the river down to Drogheda and beyond that to the sea, though dredging may have been necessary to allow them to cross the bar at the end of the estuary.

The canal by-passes the bridge at Oldbridge, the only bridge for vehicular traffic to cross the river between Slane and Drogheda. The present structure, of latticed ironwork on heavy limestone piers, replaced a much older one at the site; it dates back only to 1869, and is thus more than a decade younger than the great railway viaduct at Drogheda.

Fig. 55: The oats and wheat mill at Monknewtown, shown shortly before it became idle and was offered for sale in the Incumbered Estates Court in 1856. It is a fine example of nineteenth-century industrial architecture in Ireland.

81

The northern end of the bridge opens onto the bottom of King William's Glen, a romantically leafy road which has echoes of the hooves and drums of King William's army as one part of it marched down the glen on that fateful day in July 1690. The other part of the army went above a ravine a kilometre and a half to the west, then upstream to cross the Boyne at the ford of Rossnaree. The Stuart King James II was on the southern side, near Donore. The Prince of Orange, though he had been hit in the shoulder by a ball from the opposite bank and though his horse got temporarily bogged down in the river, was able to cross near Yellow Island, just below the bridge – with consequences that still reverberate today (see page 180). To mark William's victory, an obelisk (see fig. 119, page 180) was erected in 1736 on a tall plinth on a prominent rock below the bridge; it was illustrated in Wright's *Louthiana* (1748) and was the subject of other engravings and paintings. Wilde, who also illustrated it, was still apparently able to cross the ford in his day. According to Isaac Butler in 1744, the inscription on the plinth ran:

> Sacred to the Glorious memory of King William III who on the 1st July 1690 passed the river near this place to attack James II at the head of a popish army advantageously posted on the south side of it and did on that day by a successful battle secure to us and to our posterity our liberties and our religion. In consequence of this action James II left this Kingdom and fled to France. This memorial of our deliverance was erected in the 9th year of the reign of King George II, the first stone being laid by Lionel Sackville, Duke of Dorset, Lord Lieutenant of the Kingdom of Ireland, MDCCXXXVI.

No wonder, then, that this fine but politically all too sensitive monument – with an inscription like that! – was blown sky-high on the Feast of the Assumption in August 1923.

Drogheda

From here onwards the Boyne is tidal.

The river now passes under the new M1 motorway toll-bridge that was opened in the summer of 2003. The preparations for the roads to serve the motorway on either side have scalped swathes of Louth and Meath countryside that are irreplaceable, though they have also brought to light some Bronze Age structures which demonstrate that the Boyne Valley was not as depopulated during this period as people had hitherto believed. Off to the left, six and a half kilometres north, lies Monasterboice, with two of the best-preserved of Ireland's High Crosses; there is more detail on these in the next chapter (see page 141).

But our goal here is Drogheda, the largest and most extensive town on the Boyne, and one full of history – a history that includes a shocking massacre which has gone down in folk memory as one of the greatest injustices wrought by the English in Ireland.

Going under the Bridge of Peace, constructed as part of a by-pass scheme, we are immediately struck by the tall mound of Millmount on the right-hand side (fig. 56). It is capped by a well-preserved round tower that was part of a system of fortifications erected along the east coast of Ireland (and elsewhere) to defend the country against the threat of a Napoleonic invasion. This tower is atop a mound that could well be another Passage Grave *à la* Newgrange on a prominent knoll overlooking the Boyne, or could have been a Norman motte set up by Hugh de Lacy when granted the Lordship of Meath in 1172 – or both. John Bradley, in his article on the topography and layout of medieval Drogheda, published in the *County Louth Archaeological and Historical Journal* in 1978, argues that the Vikings probably never used this area as any kind of permanent base, because the presence of powerful Irish kings at Knowth, not far upstream, would have prevented them putting

Fig. 56: Millmount dominates Drogheda on the southern bank of the Boyne. Its recently restored tower, which provides a wonderful panorama of the town, was built in the early years of the nineteenth century to help protect the country from a potential invasion by Napoleon.

Fig. 57: Catholic and Protestant church-spires vie for attention above the rooftops of Drogheda, north of the Boyne.

down any lasting roots here. As part of the town's Millennium Commemoration, the tower was splendidly restored and given its uppermost storey. From its windows you have a series of superb views over the town (fig. 57) and its port – as well as of the Museum of the Old Drogheda Society, which is where tickets for the tower visit may be purchased. Both buildings formed part of Richmond Barracks, further houses of which have been cleverly turned into craftshops, a restaurant and other things.

The museum is the most extensive – and one of the few – in the whole Boyne Valley. It concentrates on the rich history of the town through objects either long-known or recently discovered. Tiles unearthed in the old Magdalene Friary and fragments of pottery from Ireland, England, France, Spain and Germany that have come to light in excavations in James Street and elsewhere are on display in the basement, along with various kitchen utensils, old telephones, and a coracle by Michael O'Brien of Oldbridge, the last man who made them.

Milling, the railways and the port of Drogheda all come in for their share of the museum's limelight, but the most valuable and important items in the collection are the Guild and Trade banners, the only surviving examples in the country, many of them painted by William Reynolds (1842–1881), who lived at Oldbridge although, like his schoolmate and contemporary John Boyle O'Reilly (see page 78), he was born at Dowth. It was the purpose of the Guilds to control trade in particular items for their members within a particular area. Their history in Drogheda goes back to 1307, and there were a great number of them here, as evidenced by the banners. They show the Guilds' coats-of-arms and their mottoes – for example, 'We are but one' for the weavers and 'Prepare the way to heaven' for the shoemakers! There is a splendid one, dated 1833, for the Boyne

84

salmon fishermen (fig. 58), with the Maiden's Tower at Mornington (see page 93) in the foreground and, in the background, a train passing over the great Boyne Viaduct. Photographs of town charters granted by James II and William III show what treasures the Corporation preserves; these also include a sword and sheath as well as the mace made by the Dublin silversmith Thomas Bolton in 1699/1700 and presented to the town by King William III.

The location of Millmount, with its presumed Norman motte, is significant because it was a strategic high point which looked over what was the lowest crossing point of the Boyne – the *Átha* or ford, which gives the town its slightly paradoxical sounding name of Droichead Atha (the bridge of the ford). Here, eight kilometres upstream from where the river finally joins the Irish Sea, was where the main road going up the east coast crossed the Boyne. This gave the Norman Walter de Lacy an obvious reason to found a town and a port, which by tradition he did in 1194 – an event commemorated by a special postage stamp marking the town's eight-hundredth anniversary (fig. 59, page 86). When he bestowed his charter on the town he granted each burgess a plot with a frontage 50 ft wide and free access along the Boyne as high upstream as the castle he was in the process of building at Trim.

In the medieval period the town had a twofold division, with the river acting as both dividing line and link. There was one town south of the river, where Millmount lies, and another north of the river; the division is still reflected in the two parishes – in both the Catholic Church and the Church of Ireland – of St Mary's and St Peter's. Each port was governed by a different family – the de Lacys for the south and the de Verdons for the north. It is widely believed that it was a de Verdon who founded the northern town but,

Fig. 58: The Old Drogheda Society's Museum at Millmount has the most extensive collection of Guild and Trade banners, the best of which is that of the Boyne Fishermen, shown plying their trade on the riverbank below the town, as a train passes over the Boyne Viaduct in the background. It was painted by William Reynolds in 1873,

because a de Lacy seems to have founded the two main churches, one in each of the respective halves, John Bradley is of the opinion that Walter de Lacy founded both towns. It was not until 1412 that the two sides decided to sink their differences and create a unified administrative whole.

Each part of the town, north and south, had its own town wall, that on the north being about twice the size of that on the southern bank; the two combined made Drogheda one of the largest walled towns in Ireland. The best bits of the wall to survive are in the southern part, particularly along the southern boundary of the churchyard of St Mary – the church itself, dating from the early nineteenth century, is long deconsecrated and now serves other uses. The low wall on the eastern side overlooks a steep valley which obviously gave added protection. This it successfully did during the medieval period, but it was not enough to stop the Commonwealth's Lord Protector, Oliver Cromwell, who battered the wall from the far side with his cannon on 10 September 1649, when the town – defended for King Charles I by Sir Arthur Aston – finally fell at the third assault. It is reckoned that two or three thousand defenders, including Aston himself, were put to the sword on Cromwell's orders, and an untold number of others sent off to slavery in Barbados. The slaughter has left an exceedingly bitter taste behind it in Irish folk tradition.

In 1689–90 the town was defended for another Stuart king – James II – by Lord Magennis of Iveagh, but equally to no avail, though this time it was taken without any massacre. A decade later the town had obviously recovered sufficiently for an English traveller, John Dunton, to write that Drogheda was a 'handsome, clean, English-like town and (except for Dublin) the best I have seen in Ireland'. Probably in the year before Dunton's visit the English artist Francis Place came to the town and gave us our earliest drawings of it – some from a distance, including one of St Mary's Church, others of individual buildings, particularly Sunday's Gate, a part of the town defences which no longer survives.

Talking probably of that part of Drogheda north of the Boyne, the *Parliamentary Gazetteer* of 1846 paints a picture of a town having a mixture of ruins and recent architecture representing 'a medley compound of the present and the past, of young expectations and extinguished hopes'. A memory of the 'stores and dwellings' described by the *Gazetteer* was the half-timbered house built by Nicholas Bathe in 1570 and illustrated in the *Dublin Penny Journal* of 15 September 1832 (fig. 60) – eight years after it had become so decrepit that it had had to be taken down; it can be seen to have had very intricately detailed panelling.

While Christine Casey and Alistair Rowan in their *North Leinster* volume complain that the twentieth century was not kind to Drogheda, in letting buildings such as the Drogheda Grammar School and Singleton House go to ruin, they also show its 'young expectations', complimenting the West End Arcade, a shopping development at the back of No. 82 West Street designed in 1984 for Malachy McCloskey by Patrick Shaffrey, making imaginative use of the old back gardens of the Georgian houses in Fair Street – an instance of 'courageous planning and enlightened design' that, according to Casey and Rowan, gives hope for Drogheda's future. But the twentieth century was indeed kind to Drogheda, providing it with the artist Nano Reid (1905–1981), and Dr T. K. Whitaker, who went to school there and was named Greatest Living Irishman in 2002.

The modern Catholic Church of St Mary's, giving onto the present Dublin road in the southern half of the town, is one of the two large Gothic Revival churches which, in

Fig. 59: A postage stamp was issued in 1994 to commemorate the eight-hundredth anniversary of the foundation of Drogheda.

the view of the town's architectural historian William Garner, are among the finest of their kind in the country.

The Boyne was not just the dividing line between northern and southern parts of the town, between the parishes of St Mary and St Peter, and between de Lacy and de Verdon territory. It was also where the medieval archbishops of Armagh – who lived in fear and dread of their native Irish dean and chapter – decided to base themselves at the very southern end of their diocese, with a palace in Termonfeckin. They were doubtless partially responsible for the fact that six Irish parliaments were convened in Drogheda between 1441 and 1494, of which that of 1465 was notable for passing an act setting up a university here, 'where may be made bachelors, masters and doctors in all sciences and faculties, as at Oxford'. Had this plan been implemented, Drogheda would have been a century ahead of Dublin. Another parliament, in 1467, attainted – and had beheaded – Thomas, seventh Earl of Desmond; but the most regrettable of all was that of 1494, which enacted the notorious Poynings' Law extending all the English Statutes to Ireland, and binding Ireland legislatively to London's whim.

Within the walls of the town were a number of religious institutions of which some remnants survive. Perhaps the most dominating medieval religious monument is the Magdalene Tower on top of the hill overlooking the northern part of the town. It is the only part remaining of a Dominican friary that stood just within the northern extremity of the

Fig. 60: The last of its kind, this decorative wooden house in Drogheda was built in 1570 by Nicholas Bathe, and was fortunately recorded before it was demolished in 1824. One inscribed beam from the shop-front has been preserved, however, and is now on display in the National Museum in Dublin.

87

Fig. 61: The aisle of the old abbey of St Mary d'Urso inside Drogheda's west gate is now a public thoroughfare that deserves greater respect than it has got since Petrie had his drawing of it engraved around 1820.

Province of Leinster.

Engraved by J.Greig, from a Drawing by Geo. Petrie, for the Excursions through Ireland.

ST MARY'S CHURCH, DROGHEDA, Co. of LOUTH.

wall; the tower would have acted as a useful lookout post to warn of any impending danger. Within these long-gone friary walls, Niall Óg O'Neill submitted to King Richard II in 1395. The other survival is the Abbey and Hospital of St Mary d'Urso (fig. 61), just inside the western extremity of the town wall, not far from the demolished West Gate, in the northern part of the town. It was founded around 1206 by one Urso de Swemele as a hospital for the poor, probably one of the first of its kind in the country. The whole length of the church is now a street for motorised traffic, giving rise to the apt quip that it is 'Ireland's only drive-in friary'. Not far away is Barlow House in Fair Street, one of many converted Georgian houses that give the town a distinctive flavour and bid fair to rival some of Dublin's Georgian townhouses. Having acted for many years as a Garda barracks, it has been refurbished and, as recently as February 2003, was opened by Her Excellency Mary McAleese, President of Ireland, as a new Arts complex for the town. The Tholsel, now replaced by a bank on the corner of Shop Street and West Street, was another Georgian structure; it was built by George Darley, one of a family of well-known builders-cum-architects who made their influence felt far beyond the boundaries of their native town.

It was Hugh Darley who built the Church of Ireland Parish Church of St Peter (see page 184) on the site of a massive earlier church dedicated to the Prince of Apostles, some fragments of which still lie around. Its finest memorial monument is to be found outside, near the northeastern corner of the churchyard, probably having been brought here after the medieval church was demolished. It is a double-cadaver effigy, monumental in size, showing two half-decomposed bodies, each in a shroud, probably representing Edmund Goldyng and one of his wives; it dates from about the early sixteenth century. Its gruesomeness is intended to remind us of our own mortality; such effigies are usually accompanied by an inscription saying, in effect, 'I was as you are, and as I am so you shall be.' The vast slab originally lay flat, supported by tomb-surrounds, one of which – showing angels carrying the Goldyng coat-of-arms – is let into the wall close by alongside another stone which has unidentified armorial bearings and did not belong to the tomb.

The Catholic church of St Peter, in West Street, is the other of the two that William Garner classified as among the finest Gothic Revival churches in the country. This one was built in 1880 by O'Neill and Byrne. The west transept is a special chapel dedicated to St Oliver Plunkett, whose head is preserved in the church. He was condemned to death on a trumped-up charge of treason, and hanged, drawn and quartered at Tyburn in 1681. He was canonised in 1975 – one of the few Irish saints ever to have been formally honoured in this way.

Drogheda's most important medieval monument – because of its uniqueness – is St Laurence's Gate (see fig. 107, page 163). In truth, the ivied Butter Gate, on the northern side of the river, is the only gate surviving from the town's medieval walls, because St Laurence's is, technically speaking, not a gate at all – although it did let people through its portal. It is more correctly a barbican; it stood outside the moat surrounding the town walls, in front of and as an outer protection for the actual gate of the same name, which no longer exists but stood across the road from the way leading to the Hospital of St Laurence. The barbican has two short, unequal round towers, each of four storeys linked by an internal flight of steps and joined by a crenellated parapet at the top. Dating from around the middle of the thirteenth century, St Laurence's Gate has no equal in Ireland and only a very few in England.

The road leading out from the barbican would have viewed the ships coming up the Boyne to the port of Drogheda which, in the Middle Ages, would have been protected on both banks by the town walls. The town's main import in medieval times was wine, brought from Bordeaux and other parts of southwestern France by a fleet, of which some vessels would have been Drogheda-based. Iron and salt were also brought in by sea. Exports, particularly to places like Chester, included corn and victuals; specific mention is also made of Boyne salmon. Drogheda was thus a booming town in the Middle Ages, building its ships, milling with water from the Boyne, and using a windmill that once stood on the top of Millmount. Its craftsmen and masons must have been famous; they are recorded as

The Boyne Valley

Fig. 62: This view of Drogheda north of the Boyne, showing the spire of St Peter's as well as St Laurence's Gate on the right, dates from around 1790 and is preserved on page 37 of the album numbered 1976 TX in the collection of the National Library in Dublin.

having worked at castle-building in the neighbouring county of Down and even as far away as Roscommon. All this from a town that during this period is unlikely to have had more than about 5,000 inhabitants.

The Darleys obviously kept up the strong masonry traditions of the Middle Ages, and they helped make Drogheda into a town of charm in the eighteenth and nineteenth centuries (figs. 62–63), its streets lined with some of the fine Georgian buildings mentioned above. Francis Johnston added to the attraction with his early-nineteenth-century corn market.

The prosperity which all of these buildings document was greatly reinforced by the arrival of the railway, which made Drogheda an important hub on the route from Dublin to

Fig. 63: Executed in a more painterly, but perhaps less architecturally accurate, fashion, this fine view of Drogheda as seen from the approach road from Dublin may be by the well-known landscape painter William Ashford (1746–1824), and is now in a private collection.

Belfast. The first trains started arriving from Dublin in 1844, and the line from Drogheda to Dundalk was opened from a temporary station at Newfoundwell in 1849.

The problem for passengers wanting to get from Dublin to Dundalk was that they had to dismount on the southern side of the Boyne, then take a cab across the river and up the other side to continue on their journey by another train. This difficulty was finally surmounted in 1855 with the completion of the Viaduct (fig. 64), not just Drogheda's but Ireland's greatest piece of industrial architecture, which helped the trains go through straight from Dublin to Dundalk and then on to Belfast. Its creator was Sir John MacNeill (1793–1880), who came from Dundalk and was a pupil of Thomas Telford in England. The bridge has twelve massive limestone arches on the south side of the river and three on the north, the two groups being joined by a lattice girder span of almost 70 m where the bridge crosses the river, with two subsidiary spans on either side of 43 m each. In 1932, the original wrought-ironwork for the central section was replaced in steel with an arched top cord to cater for faster and heavier trains. Crossing the bridge and looking down the 30 m to the water below is one of the more dizzying and dazzling experiences in the Boyne Valley before the river runs its last few kilometres to the sea.

Fig. 64: Sir John MacNeill's Viaduct was completed in 1855 to enable passengers to travel by train between Dublin and Belfast without having to dismount and cross the Boyne by carriage. It is arguably the finest piece of Victorian industrial architecture in Ireland.

Fig. 65: Beaulieu House, long thought to date from the 1660s but now ascribed to the second decade of the eighteenth century, is located some miles downstream from Drogheda near the Boyne's northern bank – and is one of the finest mansions along the whole length of the river.

The estuary and the sea

About three kilometres below the Viaduct the Boyne begins to expand into mudflats with plenty of interesting wildlife. Slightly inland from the left-hand (Louth) bank is one of the earliest mansions still inhabited in Ireland – Beaulieu (fig. 65), built by the Tichbourne family. Traditionally, it has been ascribed to Sir Henry Tichbourne who died in 1667, and who had been a Royalist in the Confederate war of the 1640s, before being made a marshal of the Irish army when Charles II was restored to the English throne in 1660. But recently uncovered correspondence of his grandson, another Henry, created Baron Ferrard of Beaulieu in 1718, makes it likely that much, if not indeed all, of the house is much later, dating perhaps from the decade when the Baron was ennobled. Certainly, the house is one of the Boyne's most remarkable residential neighbours, with a striking two-storey-tall hall with trophies of Lord Ferrard's father and mother, together with the coat of arms conferred on him in 1718.

In the grounds, with interesting gardens, there is a church, leaning against one wall of which is yet another remarkable cadaver effigy (fig. 66), single and much smaller than that in St Peter's churchyard in Drogheda, but for all that much more animated in its gruesome carving of worms, toads, lizards and newts. According to the late Miss Helen Roe, it dates probably from the late fifteenth or early sixteenth century.

The river has long formed a navigable channel through the mudflats, carefully buoyed with beacons to guide the sizeable ships which ply up and down to Drogheda. At the river's mouth near Mornington are two monuments, the taller of which is the Maiden's Tower (fig. 67), 20 m high and built before 1744, when Isaac Butler described it much as it is today. The tradition that it gets its name from the Maiden Queen Elizabeth I may be taken with a grain or drain of salt water, though nothing is actually known about the history of the tower which could give any better explanation or shed any light on when it was built. Given its position as guardian of the Boyne's entry to the ocean, its function as a beacon, if not a lighthouse, for incoming craft is fairly obvious, and the smaller, phallic-looking monument close by may even have served the same function of mouth-marker before the larger tower was built.

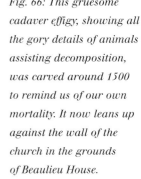

Fig. 66: This gruesome cadaver effigy, showing all the gory details of animals assisting decomposition, was carved around 1500 to remind us of our own mortality. It now leans up against the wall of the church in the grounds of Beaulieu House.

Fig. 67: The Maiden's Tower at Mornington was doubtless designed to assist mariners to find and navigate the mouth of the Boyne. It was built some three or four centuries ago.

The nearest village to them is Mornington, which is said to derive from 'Marinerstown', and to have given its name to the title of the Wellesley family of Dangan Castle (see page 34).

Another small community nearby is Colp, where the Church of Ireland church houses a small High Cross dating from around the ninth or tenth century. The name 'Colp' preserves the old Irish name Inbher Colptha, and it was here that St Patrick landed on his way to do combat with the druids of King Lóegaire. It has even older associations, if we are to believe O'Reilly's *Dictionary of Irish Writers* (1820), which says it was also the landing place of Amergin, son of Míl Espáine, the man from whom the Milesian Gaels of Ireland are said to be descended. Míl and his sons Amergin, Heber, Heremon and Ir came to take Ireland from its prehistoric inhabitants, the famed Tuatha Dé Danann. The newcomers marched to Tara, where the three existing Kings of Ireland demanded that the Milesians withdraw from Ireland for three days on the pretext that the kings should be allowed time to make up their minds as to whether they would fight or submit to the Milesian yoke. The Dé Danann believed the Milesians would be unable to withstand the enchantments of their druids, and so would not be able to land a second time. The Milesians had gone out over only nine waves to sea when the Dé Danann druids cast their spells to churn up the waters so that everything at the bottom of the sea was raised to its surface and the Milesian fleet was dispersed – but only temporarily. When the invaders finally landed again, the first among them to set foot on the soil of Ireland was the poet Amergin, who thereupon intoned the following mystical poem of rhetoric, claiming to have divine power of transformation, and identifying himself with nature and the environment in its various forms and shapes:

> *I am a wind at sea,*
> *I am a wave of the sea,*
> *I am the roaring of the sea,*
> *I am seven battalions,*
> *I am an ox in strength,*
> *I am a bird of prey on the cliff,*
> *I am a ray of the sun,*
> *I am an intelligent navigator,*
> *I am a boar of fierceness,*
> *I am a salmon in a river,*
> *I am a lake on a plain,*
> *I am an effective artist,*
> *I am a giant with a sharp sword hewing down an army,*
> *I am gods in the power of transformation.*

This was, according to the pseudo-historical tradition of around a thousand years ago, the first poem ever to be recited on Erin's soil, and, in the view of Mícheál Mac Liammóir, perhaps the first to be declaimed anywhere in northern Europe.

It is perhaps appropriate that it is at this momentous spot where both Amergin and St Patrick are thought to have landed that this mythical incantatory poem was created – just where the Boyne's fresh waters and Ireland's green land meet the salt of the Irish Sea. As I hope this chapter will have shown, the river and its surroundings still proudly retain that poetry.

*Fig. 68: Jan de Fouw's
coloured etching of a salmon
is one of a set of fourteen
designed to illustrate* The
Song of Amergin, *said to be
the first poem ever recited on
Irish soil – and therefore the
origin of Ireland's literary
tradition – after Amergin
is alleged to have made his
first landing at the mouth
of the Boyne.*

Chapter 2

Treasures of the Boyne Valley

Ireland's oldest man-made artefact

Not only the Boyne Valley's but Ireland's oldest known artefact was discovered by the late Frank Mitchell (fig. 69) some thirty years ago at Mell, only a kilometre or so northwest of Drogheda. Here the local cement factory operated a quarry to such a depth that gazing down into it could easily induce a sense of dizziness in anyone susceptible to heights. Digging downwards exposed various levels of till, with gravels containing chalk and flints. Professor Mitchell's ever-inquiring mind led him to gather some of the latter to determine their age. He brought them back to his laboratory to examine them and, to his surprise, he found that one of them was actually man-made. Nothing of that period – around quarter of a million years ago – had ever been found before in Ireland. Many had looked for traces of Old Stone Age (Palaeolithic) man in Ireland, particularly in the areas along the south coast that had not been covered by the glaciers and where humans could have gained an early foothold in the country, but all to no avail. A Palaeolithic stone axe had been found on the Aran Islands, but there had never been any satisfactory explanation as to how it could have got there in the Old Stone Age.

Fig. 69: Frank Mitchell, shown here in a portrait by David Hone that hangs in Trinity College, Dublin, where he was professor. He was the man who discovered the Palaeolithic flint deep down in the quarry at Mell. One of Ireland's last great polymaths, he contributed greatly to the public's appreciation of the geology and archaeology of the Boyne Valley.

Fig. 70: The flint flake found at Mell, outside Drogheda, was made over 300,000 years ago, making it the oldest man-made artefact known from Ireland. It was probably not made in Ireland, however, as it was most likely brought to County Louth by marine currents. It is now in the National Museum in Dublin.

Here, though, was the first Palaeolithic flint to be discovered in a reliable Irish context (fig. 70) – a slightly rolled flake with a maximum width of 8.5 cm, a piece of waste stone struck from a larger core and of a kind known from Old Stone Age contexts in Britain. Being a consummate and careful scientist, Mitchell did not get so carried away by the magnitude of his discovery as to claim he had come across the first traces of human habitation in Ireland. Realising that the flint had been rolled, he explained its presence at Mell in terms of its having been brought there by marine currents, which had transported the gravel it was found in from somewhere in the Irish Sea area that, in the Old Stone Age, had not been under water. His sober judgment was that 'the occurrence of this worked flint in County Louth cannot be claimed to demonstrate the presence of Palaeolithic man in Ireland, but it does suggest that in Britain he wandered sufficiently far to the west to reach the basin of the Irish Sea'.

The Mesolithic

Much of the first half of the period that human beings have been present in Ireland – from about 8000 BC to about 4000 BC – was taken up with the Mesolithic or Middle Stone Age. Living conditions were not easy, and life expectancy was short. To get meat, our ancestors had to find and then trap animals on the hoof, and they would have had to change the location of their camp to wherever the chase led them. At this stage, the great Irish elk was becoming extinct, if it was not already so, but red deer would have been on the menu, and wild – but not domestic – pig is known to have been eaten by the Mesolithic population in Ireland. Their houses were of the flimsiest: a couple of rods deftly woven to create a hemispherical dome which would have been covered by sods to keep rain off and heat in, though winters were probably warmer than they are now. One source of nourishment we know these people had was fish and, given the Boyne's richness in salmon, it would be surprising if the men and women of Ireland's Middle Stone Age were not, at least metaphorically, casting their rods beside the river's banks. They probably didn't have hooks, so catching salmon – or any other species of fish – can't have been an easy job.

It is surprising, then, that so few traces of these Mesolithic peoples have been found in the Boyne Valley, although one of their typical products, the so-called 'Bann flake' – a partially leaf-shaped flint broadly struck to provide a point at one end – has been found at Newgrange. However, because other Mesolithic stone material has been collected not far from the Tremblestown River, which drains into the Boyne not far from Trim, we may presume that Mesolithic peoples passed up the Boyne to get there. It is likely that future surface collecting, and possibly even excavation, will produce more evidence that these people hunted along the Boyne. It should be pointed out, however, that the level of the sea may have risen since the Middle Stone Age, and that there may have been camps – or perhaps even slightly more permanent settlements – clustered around the mouth of the Boyne that have since been submerged.

The Neolithic, or New Stone Age

The east coast of Ireland from Antrim to Wexford was the obvious landing point for anyone down the centuries coming to Ireland from the neighbouring island to the east. It is still a matter of debate among scholars as to when the landbridge which once joined the two islands finally collapsed, but it is becoming more and more likely that it had disappeared before the Mesolithic, and certainly before Neolithic man first set foot in Ireland. Simple log-boats or dugouts would have been used to cross the North Channel or the Irish Sea, bringing families and – when the Neolithic dawned sometime around 4000 BC – their corn- or barley-seed and trussed-up animals. Given that the landscape would have then been more densely covered by tree and scrub than it is today, rivers would have been the easiest way to penetrate into the interior in search of game or a place to settle permanently and rear domesticated stock. The Neolithic peoples would have sought out good land to start cultivating crops as soon as they had chopped down trees and created forest clearances where their flocks could safely graze. Of the locations along the east coast where any kind of sizeable rivers flowed into the Irish Sea in low-lying countryside, the area between the Mournes and the Dublin mountains offered some of the best landing opportunities.

The Vikings may have made Dublin the future capital, but the Neolithic people chose the Boyne as their most significant point of access; it is worth a thought that, had it not been for the Vikings moving on to Dublin after their first temporary settlement in Annagassan in County Louth, Drogheda might now be the capital of Ireland if large ocean-going vessels could reach it. We can reasonably claim that it was the area just upstream from this town that can be awarded the title of 'Cradle of Irish Civilisation'. This is not to say that the Boyne Valley was the first place in Ireland where Neolithic families burgeoned, for we know of earlier settlements elsewhere in the country, but it is the place where these Stone Age people created some of the most remarkable monuments of the period anywhere in Europe.

Passage Graves in the Bend of the Boyne –
A sacred and sepulchral landscape

New Stone Age people appear to have spread westwards across Europe from the Fertile Crescent of Mesopotamia, bringing with them new farming techniques, better-bred stock and the notion of permanent settlement, though the idea of living in villages does not seem to have fired the imagination of those who populated Western Europe. When they reached Ireland they would have found families of earlier Mesolithic populations scattered around the forests and scrubland, with whom they would, in time, have interbred, so that by the end of the Stone Age the Irish population was a successful blend of old and new, strong enough to supply the basic and important gene-pool for the people of Ireland today.

Precisely when the transition from a hunter–gatherer economy to one of settled agriculture occurred in Ireland is a matter for conjecture, but sometime around 4000 BC would probably be a fair estimate. Obviously the transition did not happen overnight, and there must have been a considerable overlap in both time and way of life before the Mesolithic population was finally convinced of the benefits of the new farming ways and blended with the incoming population. The newcomers are unlikely to have constituted an invasion, but rather would have arrived one family at a time in their precarious craft across the North Channel or the Irish Sea, each time landing where wind and current chanced to aid their rowing capabilities. The visibility of Antrim from the Mull of Kintyre, in Scotland, might argue that this shortest route was the first to have been traversed, but this by no means excludes the possibility – indeed, the likelihood – of crossings farther south having been used as well.

The low-lying land around the estuary of the Boyne would probably have been an easy landfall, and the Boyne offered one of the best fish supplies of any of the rivers flowing into the Irish Sea, plus sediment enough to help in the cultivation of crops. Clearing some of the well-wooded surroundings must have been a challenge, but those surroundings would also have been a source of wild meat.

We know surprisingly little about the earliest farmers in the Boyne Valley, because their homes have largely managed to elude us. Indeed, there is not much to show above ground for the hundreds of years that passed between the first arrival of Neolithic inhabitants and their starting to build houses for the dead in the form of the Passage Graves, which were so much more permanent than the small wooden dwellings of Meath's early farmers. Evidence from beneath the surface, however, shows that people started settling in the Bend of the Boyne by about 3800 BC, building rectangular houses at Knowth and using round-bottomed, shouldered, undecorated pottery of a kind also found under one of the 'satellite' Passage Graves west of the main mound at Newgrange. The Knowth houses, excavated by George Eogan and Helen Roche, were built with upright wooden posts; possibly there were also plank walls at ground level. One of the Knowth houses was partially built over when the great Passage Grave mound was constructed, but there is no evidence to show that house- and tomb-builders were the same people – there may have been a gap of many generations between them. No greater contrast could be imagined than that between these meagre rectangular houses and the curving kerb and circumference of the massive stone-built mounds that constitute the three great Passage Tomb cemeteries of Dowth, Knowth and Newgrange (fig 71).

The term 'Passage Grave' is used to describe round mounds of earth and stone which have, typically, a long passage leading into a burial chamber located somewhat off-centre.

Fig. 71: A recent early-morning aerial view of Newgrange shows the white-fronted mound to be accompanied by a satellite tomb, and a large wooden circle in the bottom left-hand quadrant.

Such a description could almost equally apply to the Egyptian Pyramids, except for the roundness and the fact that the latter are, of course, built entirely of stone and house a single deified pharaoh – unlike the Irish Passage Graves, which were for multiple burials, like the family vaults still in use today. But for us a more significant difference is that some of the Boyne tombs, and others elsewhere in Ireland (such as in County Sligo), are likely to have been built a couple of centuries or more before the Pyramids. So also are some of the great Temples of Malta and the Passage Graves of Brittany, and the distribution of such tombs along the whole Atlantic coast of Europe, from southern Spain to the Orkneys and beyond, shows just how extensive the spread of the Passage Grave idea was in the Europe of the fourth millennium BC. At present it would appear that the Breton examples are the oldest in Western Europe.

We need not envisage a whole flotilla of Passage Grave practitioners setting forth from Brittany like missionaries to bring the idea of the latest mortuary practices and architecture to Ireland's shores! All you needed was a handful of people zealously promoting an idea which was bound to appeal to the egos and ancestral pride of the resident local population; the ancestors of those who built the Irish Passage Graves were probably resident in the country for generations. Even the idea of building megalithic tombs was not necessarily new to Ireland: Passage Graves were probably preceded by dolmens and so-called court tombs, which are not represented in the Boyne Valley.

We cannot establish which were the first Irish Passage Graves, although we can say with reasonable probability that the Boyne Valley tombs were not the beginning of the series but its zenith – after which came a period of comparative decline, represented by the Mound of the Hostages on the Hill of Tara (see fig. 85, page 124), among others. Some Passage Graves are found individually, but most tend to be clustered together into cemetery groupings, often – though not invariably – located on hilltops. The reason was presumably that they could thereby be seen from afar, thus raising their builders in the estimation of the surrounding population and glorifying the homes of the ancestral dead, to whom their descendants could point as justification for retaining a claim on the lands that they held.

The Boyne Valley tombs are not exactly on hilltops, but they nevertheless form a very dominant feature in the landscape, visible at a distance no matter from which angle you view them and, if the reconstruction of Newgrange be correct, glistening white (see fig. 50, page 75) on sunny and even dull days, like India's marble Taj Mahal. The grouping of three such outstanding monuments as Knowth, Dowth and Newgrange make the lower Boyne Valley, between Slane and Drogheda, into something of a special, sacred, ritual landscape comparable to not one but three cathedrals in a single city. It has in fact been suggested that the feat of constructing these great tombs might be compared to the building of cathedrals in the Gothic period or, to extend the analogy, sending rockets to outer space today, given that the Passage Grave builders had only very primitive technology at their disposal and yet managed to build some of the world's first great architectural masterpieces, with decoration which would be hard to better on the European continent at the time.

The three tombs are each different, and it is worth while examining them in greater detail one by one, in alphabetical order, to see what remarkable qualities each reveals.

Dowth

Dowth is the farthest of the three mounds down the river, less than a kilometre from the bank, and the first to be encountered on the approach upstream from Drogheda. Seemingly less prominent than the others, because partially obscured by trees, it is in fact of much the same size – the diameter of its kerb, at about 76 m, being virtually identical with that at Newgrange. In shape, however, Dowth bears a greater resemblance to Knowth, in that its outline was more rounded – a circumstance later somewhat altered by the placing of rubble on top when the site was excavated at the end of the Famine years, in 1847–8.

The earliest sketches of Dowth exaggerate the height over the width when compared with what we see today. The very first (fig. 72), done in 1775 by Gabriel Beranger (preserved as page 5 of the Royal Irish Academy's manuscript 3.C.30), shows a curious and very much later structure on top. Beranger described this as a 'temple' intended as a gala room and 'having a gallery which is to serve as orchestra'. But it would appear from Dean Anthony Cogan's *The Diocese of Meath: Ancient and Modern* (1868) that its somewhat reclusive builder, John, sixth Viscount Netterville, used it to follow the Catholic mass

Fig. 72: Gabriel Beranger's watercolour of the large Passage Grave at Dowth in 1775, now preserved as page 5 of the Royal Irish Academy's manuscript 3.C.30, shows a 'temple' on top that was used as a music room before it was removed during excavations in the 1840s.

celebrated in the old chapel nearby on Sunday mornings when it would not have been appropriate for him, as a Protestant, to be seen to be participating in person. The structure survived until the mid-nineteenth century, when the excavation swept it away as the diggers dug down into the top of the mound in search of a central grave like the one that had come to light in Newgrange in 1699.

The excavators failed to find what they sought, but were compensated somewhat by discovering a miniature version of such a grave on the western side, not far from another which had already been known for a long time. The simpler of these two Passage Graves (both now locked and inaccessible), known as Dowth South, had a low kerbstone across the entrance, and consisted of a passage less than 4 m long with three large upright slabs on each side to bear the roof. By clambering over a low sill, you then reach the roughly circular burial chamber, whose twelve uprights now support a roof of concrete, although the original was probably corbelled, as at Newgrange and at one of the tombs at Knowth. A scarcely noticeable sill leads into a wedge-shaped recess or side-chamber, which must have been of great significance for the Passage Grave people; in Newgrange, as we shall see, this is the location of the greatest amount of decoration in the tomb. In the acme of all Passage Graves – the Treasury of Atreus at Mycenae – the only recess is in a similar position on the right-hand side as one enters the chamber.

It is at Dowth South that we are introduced to Passage Grave art, that is, the decoration of stones which distinguishes the Boyne Valley and Meath Passage Graves from most others of their ilk. This art consists of usually geometrical patterns, normally pecked out of the surface by a stone implement, forming a series of often random-seeming designs on some stones but also frequently united with others on the same surface. We do not know what significance these designs may have had for the builders. The only 'coherent' grouping of motifs in Dowth South is found on two stones facing the entrance at the back of the tomb. The drawings which illustrate Claire and M.J. O'Kelly's illuminating paper on Dowth (published in 1983 in the *Proceedings of the Royal Irish Academy*) indicate the association of zigzags, triangles, diamond-shapes and others on one stone, and serpentiform and angular designs on the other. The large vertical stone on the right in the side-chamber is also heavily decorated (but probably at various times) with a variety of what look like Stone Age doodlings as well as a spiral, a possible 'sun-ray' motif, and what seem like hot cross buns. Anne-Marie Moroney, who made a study of the sun shining into the chamber, has discovered that it is lit up by a wide sunbeam in winter afternoons after 3 o'clock, with the colour changing from yellow to pink around the time of the solstice and going through a spectrum from honey to a bright white by the time spring approaches at the beginning of February. She also observed that, significantly, around the time of the solstice the sun shines directly onto the lower part of the two big decorated stones at the back of the chamber – which can scarcely be a coincidence.

The same phenomenon cannot be observed in the other Dowth tomb discovered during the 1847–8 excavation, for the sun no longer shines into Dowth North thanks to, among other things, a build-up of earth outside it. The original entrance to Dowth North was destroyed many centuries ago anyway when a souterrain, or underground stone-lined passage, cut right across the mouth of the passage, coming from farther north inside the mound's ancient kerb to terminate in a beehive-like room beside the tomb entrance.

Dowth North is a much more complicated construction than its southern counterpart a mere 20 m away. It belongs to what might be called the 'classic' Passage Grave, with a plan

Fig. 73: Some of the massive kerbstones surrounding the mound at Dowth bear Passage Grave art which must have had ritual significance for its builders some five thousand years ago.

in the shape of a Latin cross (although nothing to do with Christianity). A passage about 12 m long, corresponding to the stem of the cross, leads to a central chamber from which two side-chambers veer off like arms to the right and left, and ahead is a third chamber completing the upper limb of the cross-form. Just as we shall see at Newgrange, the height of the passage rises as it proceeds inwards, and the tall stones forming the central chamber support a corbelled roof. Lying on the floor of the central chamber is a large 'basin stone', assembled at the time of the excavation from the nine fragments into which it had been shattered; from the example of Newgrange, it is more likely that this stone was set originally in one of the side-chambers, where the bones of the dead – cremated or otherwise – would have been placed.

R.H. Firth, who oversaw the mid-nineteenth-century excavation, claimed to have found half-burned animal bones here but, surprisingly, no trace of human remains – though some were recorded at Dowth in the eighteenth century. He also found two iron knives and a bronze pin, suggesting that the animal bones were remnants left by those who had built the souterrain in the late prehistoric or Early Christian period.

What makes this tomb different from all the other Passage Graves is the addition of two small chambers to the right-hand side-chamber. These have two stones decorated with concentric circles, some with lines radiating from a point at their centre. The same designs predominate on the kerbstones that originally delineated the extent of the mound. Fifty-five of these large recumbent stones are visible above ground today, of which less than a quarter are decorated, the often worn ornament on some of them proclaiming its presence only when the sun shines obliquely on the surface into which the designs have been pecked (fig. 73, page 105). The most prominently decorated stone of all, bearing a series of encircled sunbursts, is located on the eastern side of the mound opposite the two known tombs, and could mark the entrance to another tomb.

Dowth is the only one of the three great Passage Tombs of the Bend of the Boyne which was not excavated using modern methods in the twentieth century, but perhaps that is as well: more refined techniques may be applied to it in the twenty-first, and may be able to shed even more sophisticated light on the evolution of Dowth, which has hitherto remained the Cinderella of the Boyne Valley's three Passage Grave sites.

Knowth

Dowth lies at the eastern end of the low ridge of hills where the Boyne makes its bend. Knowth stands at the western end of this same ridge.

The 1960s were the decade when the archaeology of the Boyne Valley really began to buzz. With encouragement from P.J. Hartnett, archaeologist to the Irish Tourist Board, which wanted the Passage Grave at Newgrange made more accessible, Professor M.J. O'Kelly started his excavations in 1962. During the previous two years, George Eogan and G.F. Mitchell had excavated a small but highly interesting Passage Grave on the Louth side of the Boyne at Townley Hall, where Professor Mitchell lived. This grave has a series of almost concentric circular settings enclosing, near their centre, a rectangular burial chamber which did not differentiate between entrance passage and tomb. It was this excavation and its results that led Professor Eogan to focus his sights on the great mound at Knowth, where he started excavating the same year that O'Kelly began at Newgrange. Forty years on, in what must be one of Europe's longest-standing excavations, he has revealed many surprising – and, at times, highly exciting – secrets of this great Boyne Valley tumulus.

Where many would have rushed in to seek Knowth's version of the long-known tomb at Newgrange, George Eogan prepared the ground carefully by examining first what lay around the foot of the mound. He knew it was likely that there was more there than met the eye, for R.A.S. Macalister, the first professor of archaeology in University College, Dublin, had conducted a small excavation on the site in 1941 and revealed a box-shaped tomb with a passage which he had described as a 'minor grave monument'.

Little could Eogan have suspected how many more such monuments of various kinds he was to bring to light around the mound. Including Macalister's original one, the total amounted to a staggering eighteen; when first built, they must have looked like a clutch of chickens randomly spread around the base of the mother-hen mound.

Most of these satellite tombs were contained within a usually circular setting of kerbstones (fig. 74), though some had a straightened façade on either side of the tomb

Fig. 74: Satellite tombs at Knowth have been reconstructed in recent years to show what they must have originally looked like around the base of the great Passage Grave mound.

entrance. Of those which survived sufficiently well to provide Eogan with plans, the layout varied from Macalister's box-like chamber to others where the passage gradually expanded along its length and height to become the tomb, and yet a further group which resembled the classic cruciform plan encountered at Dowth North. None of these was preserved to anything like its full original height and many had been severely damaged, but a number have now been reconstructed and covered with a grassy top to allow visitors to enter and experience for themselves what it must have been like for the original builders some five thousand years ago.

One of the tombs had a stone basin of the kind already encountered at Dowth North. Finds included rather coarsely jabbed pottery bowls dubbed 'Carrowkeel ware', typical of Passage Graves but in their crudeness creating a strong contrast to the refined decoration found on some of the tomb stones. Other items which accompanied the burials – sometimes inhumed, other times cremated – include further material typical of Passage Graves such as chalk balls and a decorated bone pin.

The rather higgledy-piggledy nature of the layout and spread of these satellite tombs (fig. 75) suggests there was no predetermined planning – that they were all built just wherever there was space. The varying tomb-plans would also argue for their not having all been built at the same time, but rather that the site just 'growed and growed' as necessity arose over a number of centuries. One of them is certainly older than the main tomb, because the latter's kerb makes a detour in order to avoid it, and it is quite possible that a number of the other satellites are likewise older than the 'mother mound'. Without excavating the whole large tomb down to ground level and below – which is not envisaged – it is impossible to know whether there were originally a whole lot of other examples of the smaller tomb variety beneath it.

One of the more recent 'discoveries' George Eogan has surprised us with is, as he so pertinently put it in the title of an article published in *Antiquity* in 1998, that there was a 'Knowth before Knowth' – in other words, that there must have been another important tomb built on or near the site before the present mound was constructed. He came to this startling conclusion through studying stones within the present mound which had had their decoration hidden away and which, he believes, must have been re-used after serving initially in some earlier large and ornamented tomb. He makes the same intriguing, if as yet unproven, suggestion that some of the stones in Newgrange which likewise had their decoration hidden from view when used in the construction may also have belonged to the same hypothetical pre-Knowth tomb, located somewhere – we know not where – in the vicinity of one or other of the great tombs we see today.

It was only after a few years' work around the periphery that Eogan finally began to tackle the large mound, which is about 9 m high and covers an area of an acre and a half. It was built like a layer cake, with alternating strata of stones and sods. While the mound gives the impression of being round, the line of the kerbstones shows that it was rounded only on the northern and southern portions; elsewhere the curvature is flattened, almost forming a straight line in some places. The mound's diameter across the curved parts is marginally larger than Dowth's, but from one flattened side to the other it is slightly narrower than Dowth.

Macalister and Eogan had not been the first to excavate here since the Stone Age. Locals dug away inside the kerb during the first millennium AD to make a souterrain, just as they had done at Dowth, and the same kind of dry-stone walling used in it also appears to line a passage leading in at right-angles towards the centre of the mound. On the afternoon of 11 July 1967 Eogan began to remove earth from this passage when a cavity appeared ahead. The smallest member of the excavating team was given a torch so that he could squeeze through and find out what was inside. When he returned and said that he saw a passage that went in for twenty yards, his report was received with a mixture of delight and caution. After a little more earth had been removed, Eogan himself was able to look, and could confirm to his own satisfaction what he had been told. One after the other, the small group of excavators – including George's wife Fiona and the late Tom Fanning – crawled along the passage, under a fallen stone and through a puddle of water, before being able to stand erect again and follow the passage's rising capstones until finally coming to the centre of the tomb, where all could gaze with wonderment at the central stone basin and the decorated stones, unseen for a millennium or more. Though the dazzle of gold was naturally not present in this Stone Age tomb, the feeling of awe must have been closely akin to that experienced by Howard Carter when he discovered Tutankhamen's tomb forty-five years earlier.

What Eogan had hit upon was one of the longest Passage Graves known – more than 30 m from the inside of the kerbstone to the back of the tomb. For about seven-eighths of its length it consists of a long and narrow passage, which makes an angle to the right near the end before finally increasing in height and expanding slightly to the left to form the burial chamber, which is really just an enlargement of the passage. The basin stone had presumably once formed part of the chamber furniture, but tomb-robbers a thousand years or more ago must have tried to drag it out into the open air – and failed, for it still lies in the passage, which is as far as they were able to bring it.

Eighty uprights form the walls of passage and chamber together, though originally there would have been more near the entrance, which was demolished by the souterrain builders. Many of the stones bear pocking, but by no means all are decorated in any formal way. The

Fig. 75: Seen from the air, the satellite tombs at Knowth show no particular pattern in their spread around the main mound.

kerbstone outside the entrance to the tomb, however, gives an inkling of one of the ornamental styles found inside. It is a long, low stone covered with a whole series of boxed half-rectangles and, most significantly of all, a vertical line in the centre which, for the builders, almost certainly marked the entrance to the tomb. The same motif is found on the back-stone of the tomb, linking start and finish for a purpose we can no longer understand.

A few of the upright stones in the first three-quarters of the passage are pecked with ornament which has visible signs of zigzags, spirals and angular designs, but it is in that part of the passage after the bend – and on the upright stones that form the walls of the expanded tomb area at the end of it – that we find the most striking motifs (fig. 76). A number bear boxed circular or angular designs; of these stones the most remarkable is that beyond the first low sill-stone in the passage. Its outer face has boxed upright rectangles topped by sets of concentric circular motifs. This stone immediately caught the attention of Eogan as he eased himself along the passage for the first time, when he recognised in it the stylised form of a human figure, with two staring eyes. The design bears a curious resemblance to Edvard

Fig. 76: The almost owl-like features on one of the most remarkable decorated stones in the passage of the western tomb at Knowth may be a stark stylisation of a human face, with eyes above and mouth below.

Fig. 77: Secondary pock-dressing on a stone in the western tomb-chamber at Knowth obliterated earlier carvings and left smooth a surface that somewhat resembles a bear in shape.

Munch's *The Scream*, but Eogan was probably getting closer to its intention when he described it as a 'ghostly guardian' of the approach to the inner sanctum. The other remarkable stone is on the left-hand wall of the chamber, at right-angles to the back-stone, where extensive pocking left the central part of the stone smoothened to reveal what I always fondly imagine to be a bear with a runny nose (fig. 77)!

Before succumbing to obvious temptation and immediately starting to excavate the tomb, Eogan continued his researches inside the kerb. During the following season's campaign, he reached the opposite, eastern, side of the great mound. There he thought he had come upon another souterrain inside the kerb, and this led him to suspect there might be a second tomb here. This seemed a mere fancy, unworthy of serious consideration, as no similar instance was known among the round-mounded Irish Passage Graves. On 30 July 1968 he descended through a hole into four passages whose dry-stone walling confirmed that they belonged to one or more souterrains. Having come to a dead end in three of them, he tried the fourth. This led in towards the mound and – though progress became more difficult, uprights from each side having fallen inwards towards one another – he was able to clamber over them and come upon what he described as the most amazing sight of his life: a well-preserved cruciform Passage Tomb chamber similar to those at Dowth North and, more significantly, Newgrange – but untouched by human hand for more than a thousand years. In the light of his torch he could see a number of decorated stones and a masterly basin-stone, beautifully shaped and decorated.

It is given to few people to come across one major intact Irish Passage Grave, but no one other than George Eogan has had the joy and surprise of finding a second example in the same mound.

The two tombs are not small, like those at Dowth, and the second tomb has a passage much longer than the similar example at Newgrange as well as a chamber rivalling Newgrange's in height. The two Knowth tombs are totally different: the first has a chamber which is an expansion of the passage, and the second is cross-shaped in plan. Yet both are fitted snugly back-to-back with one another and almost meet in the centre, the gap between them being less than 10 ft (3 m). Finding two very different tomb-types under the same mound

Fig. 78: Rich decoration on the perimeter kerbstones, for which Knowth is famous, leaves us wondering what their sinuous spirals and curves meant for those who carved them.

raises the intriguing chicken-and-egg question: which came first, or were they both built at the same time? Sadly, neither tomb is accessible to the public, but it is possible to view a stretch of the passage to the eastern tomb from a recently constructed chamber in the mound.

A great number of the stones in this eastern tomb bear signs of pocking, creating a roughened surface probably by means of a pointed flint. The kerbstone outside the entrance has a series of boxed rectangles – like a pair of eyes looking out at the world as through angular spectacles and inspecting those who enter the tomb behind the central vertical line. Decoration begins to increase about two-thirds of the way along the passage, where it is difficult to make much sense out of the juxtaposition of angular and curved lines in the stones. Similar features occur on some of the stones of the highly decorated chamber walls, and one gets the impression that the artists (who almost certainly would not have regarded themselves as such) were becoming more and more adept at an ever-increasing stylisation the farther they distanced themselves from what must originally have been a realistic model for the designs, like the gradual transition from realism to abstraction in the world of painting a century ago. The chamber of this eastern tomb has a much stronger geometrical streak, with series of zigzags, positive and negative triangles, rows of diamond-shapes arranged point-to-point and even one 'rayed sun' motif, perhaps a reference to a main god worshipped by the Passage Tomb builders.

Aside from there being two great tombs under the one mound, a further feature that makes Knowth stand out among its peers is the richness of the decoration on the 123 exposed kerbstones. Here we find many of the motifs we have already encountered – zigzags, spirals, concentric circles, positive and negative diamond rows – all with various permutations and combinations, but most executed in a very competent manner by pecking

112

out the designs from the fairly smooth surface of the greywacke boulders (fig. 78). Two are particularly notable. One, numbered 13 by George Eogan, has an arrangement of diamond shapes which – as on a decorated stone at Fourknocks on the Dublin–Meath border – I can only interpret as a splendidly stylised human face with eyes and nose. Even more remarkable is the next-but-one neighbour, No. 15, which is dominated by what looks like a sundial, even having a small hole for a gnomon, which could have helped mark the times of the day. Eogan was able to establish that, when the decorated kerbstones are combined with the ornamented stones in both chambers, Knowth incorporates a quarter of all the megalithic art known anywhere in Europe, and almost half of all the known megalithic art hitherto recognised in Ireland.

Since these people were capable of creating such sophisticated patterns on stone, it comes as somewhat of a disappointment to see the generally poor quality of the pottery associated with the burials, which seem largely to have been cremations. One stunning find at Knowth, however, shows just what high-calibre goods could be deposited with the dead in Irish Passage Tombs. This is an ovoid macehead (fig. 79) discovered on the old ground level at the entrance to the right-hand recess of the eastern tomb. Carved from flint, it is perforated to hold a wooden handle, the hole serving also as the mouth for a superbly stylised face with spiralled eyes, a beard and backward-groomed hair. The sides consist of three-strand spirals curling into a centre with a modelling that looks forward to the finest Aeolian columns of classical Greece. This is a piece of stylised art which, though physically small, dwarfs in quality any grave goods from elsewhere in Ireland – indeed, from anywhere else in Europe at the time. It shows the builders of Passage Graves to have been 'giants' in achievement, in both the ingenuity of their structures and the quality of their art. We should doff our caps to Ireland's first master-craftsmen!

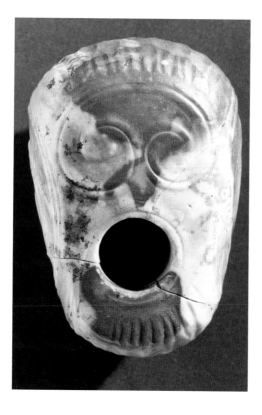

Fig. 79: The flint macehead found in the eastern tomb at Knowth bears the stylised image of a human head and shows the great artistic heights to which Stone Age craftsmen could aspire.

Newgrange

The medieval St Patrick's Purgatory on Lough Derg in County Donegal used to be Ireland's most renowned ancient site, with a fame that spread right across Europe. But its reputation has been roundly overtaken in the last three decades by Newgrange, because of the discovery that at the winter solstice the rising sun there shines into the darkest recesses of its burial chamber. Even without that unique feature, Newgrange deserved its place as one of Ireland's most significant prehistoric monuments, for it is among the world's earliest great pieces of architecture – probably older than the Pyramids, and only slightly younger than the Temples in Malta.

In early Irish mythology, Newgrange had an important role to play. It had the name of Brú na Bóinne: (*brú* is a dwelling, a hall or a mansion). It was considered to have been built by the Dagda, the good god of the Tuatha Dé Danann, a people who had occupied Ireland but had retired to the fairy mounds and forts of the island when the Gaels came and took the country from them. The Dagda was also seen as the lover of Bóann, the goddess who gave her name to the River Boyne. She was the wife of Elcmar, otherwise Nuadu, another of the Tuatha Dé Danann (when not a King of Leinster named Nechtan – see page 15), who was understood to live in Brú na Bóinne, according to the ninth-century tale *The Wooing of Etaín*. The Dagda, desiring Bóann, contrived to send Elcmar away on a journey which would have no night – for Elcmar had promised he would be back between day and night. The Dagda thereby succeeded in keeping Elcmar occupied elsewhere for more than nine months, time enough for Bóann to bear the god a son, whose name was Aongus, a symbol of the vigour of youth. To avoid Elcmar learning the truth, the Dagda brought Aongus away to another mound-owner, Midir, of Brí Leith in Longford, who fostered the boy as his own son. But one day Aongus was told by a playmate that Midir was not his father, as he had thought. He went to Midir seeking clarification, and was told who his real father was. Midir brought the boy to the Dagda, who advised Aongus to go to the Brú at Samhain (the start of winter) and threaten to kill the unarmed Elcmar. This Aongus did, although he declined to carry out the threat. In return for his life being spared, Elcmar allowed Aongus to become king of the Brú for a day and a night. Elcmar duly returned after twenty-four hours to claim his Brú and the land that belonged to it, but Aongus said the decision as to who should own it should be put to the Dagda. The latter tricked Elcmar out of his dwelling by judging that 'it is in days and nights that the world is spent', and allotting the Brú to Aongus. (Dáithí Ó hÓgáin argues that the Dagda is a deity who went underground at night to light up the darkness of the other world, and by day he lit up this 'world of the living'. His mating with Bóann thus represented the fruitful union of sun and mother earth.) By way of consolation the Dagda gave Elcmar some land at Cleiteach (Cletty) 'to the south', which has been tentatively identified as Rossnaree, on the far side of the Boyne, and the link between Newgrange as burial mound and Rossnaree as royal residence is also expressed in the tale of Cormac mac Airt (see page 76).

A twelfth-century story in *The Book of Leinster* gives an alternative version of how Aongus, the embodiment of youthful vigour, bests the ageing adult, this time in the form of his own father, the Dagda, by possessing the *Brú* for a day and a night and then refusing to give it back on the pretext that 'a day and a night' means forever.

In ancient storytelling, the Brú was seen not just as a burial site but as a place in and out of which people with supernatural qualities could come and go. According to tradition, the Brú could never be burned or harried as long as Aongus lived.

The actual mound or cairn (see figs. 50 and 71, pages 75 and 101), consisting mainly of pebbles rounded by water, is over 9 m high and flatter-topped than the other two Bend of the Boyne mounds we have seen. As with them, the mound is delimited by a kerb of large stones, 97 in total, of which a number are decorated, though not as many as at Knowth. Its diameter varies, but averages about 76 m, the reason for the variation being that the circle is flattened in its southeastern quadrant on either side of the entrance to the tomb – a feature we have encountered also at Knowth (see page 108). There is, however, a further flattened part of the circle just to the east of its northernmost point, and so we may well ask if another tomb may not lurk there, for the known chamber at Newgrange does not go into the centre of the mound but leaves room for another, back to back or at an angle to it. M.J. O'Kelly searched for a second passage, but in vain.

O'Kelly began excavating at Newgrange in 1962, when it became necessary to straighten up the inward-sloping stones of the passage to allow access to the ever-increasing numbers of tourists. This move opened the flood gates: the throngs continue today, and the rubbing of their clothes against the ornamented surfaces threatens with time to damage priceless designs that have withstood the test of millennia.

The Newgrange chamber has been known for longer than those at Dowth and Knowth, and the Newgrange entrance passage and chamber were found in the same way that one of the Dowth tombs was first exposed – through the exploitation of a ready-made quarry for road-metalling. For centuries, the downward pressure of the central stones of the mound had caused some of the peripheral material to spill out over the kerbstones, most of which thus remained covered until Professor O'Kelly's spade liberated them. However, just over three hundred years ago, in 1699, the Newgrange chamber itself was rediscovered, thus allowing people to trample the ground of both passage and chamber ever since, probably removing or destroying any small artefacts which might have survived from the Stone Age and leaving the remnants of only four burials for O'Kelly to uncover on the tomb-floor during the course of his excavations.

Today the front façade of the tomb shines with white quartz stones which were discovered in the slip of the mound, according to O'Kelly. He noted down carefully where they were found, then asked an engineer to design for him a wall of quartz above the kerbstones; his reasoning was that there must originally have been such a wall but that it fell, scattering the stones to the places where he had found them. On the basis of his report, the Commissioners of Public Works – the owners of the monument on behalf of the state – reconstructed the gleaming white wall as we see it today, though admittedly with a concrete backing lest the stones should tumble forward again. Interspersed among the quartz are large round pebbles which look like currants in a cake, just to show that this is not truly an ancient wall. However, recent work at both Newgrange and Knowth shows that not just pebbles and quartz but also other stones were brought from many miles away for use in the mounds, some from near the coast in the neighbouring county of Louth but some from at least as far away as the southern shores of County Down, the heavier ones probably being hauled upstream by raft from the rivermouth. Because it is not known exactly what the entrance to the tomb-passage looked like, the Commissioners have clad it with a limestone that is so modern-looking that no one could mistake it for the original.

The reconstruction has proved controversial over the twenty and more years of its existence. Some argue that no sensible Passage Grave builder would put up a wall of not very large stones at an angle like that, as it would be bound to fall down. Others claim that

Fig. 80: This stone, wondrously decorated with spiral and lozenge motifs, stands in front of the entrance to the Newgrange tomb. The roof-box is partially visible above the doorway.

the white stones never formed part of an upright wall at all, but rather were part of a pavement at the foot of the mound, perhaps sloped slightly upwards in sympathy with the rise of the ground on which the mound was built.

This rise is very clearly experienced as you approach the mound and, because the tumulus too is built on rising ground, the 19-m long passage necessarily slopes upwards towards the burial chamber, gaining almost 2 m in height in the process. As anyone who enters the passage today will realise, the doorway (fig. 80) is considerably shorter than the average human being passing through the portal. But the orientation of the passage was designed so that the dawning sun, as it creeps slowly above the horizon at the winter solstice, can shine through the portal for anything up to five successive days, with a midpoint on 22 December rather than on the usually celebrated festive occasion a day earlier, 21 December.

The sun's rays, shining through the doorway and following the slope of the passage, reach up only a little more than halfway along the passage's length. This was of course realised by Newgrange's builders, and so they created a narrow horizontal slit above the entrance which to this day is called by the old-fashioned term 'roof-box'. In my student days, the explanation for this unusual feature was that, after the still-surviving door of the passage had been closed behind a burial, food could be passed to the dead through the roof-box, falling down through a crack in the capstones of the passage onto the floor below. But in 1967 – the same year George Eogan discovered his first tomb at Knowth in midsummer – O'Kelly made the startling midwinter discovery that has given Newgrange an international reputation ever since. (It has to be noted that the locals seem long to have known of the phenomenon.) This was that, for a mere nineteen minutes on each of the days around the winter solstice, from 8.58 to 9.17 a.m., a pencil-thin shaft of light creeps through the roof-box to illuminate the passage at a sufficiently high level that it can actually reach beyond it and into the centre of the chamber.

Professor Tom Ray, of the Dublin Institute of Advanced Studies, discovered over a decade ago that originally the sun's rays, instead of stopping 1.8 m or so short of the backstone of the hindmost chamber, would probably have penetrated into its remotest recess, because the earth's angle of tilt was slightly different when Newgrange was built some five thousand years ago. This means that the sun then rose at a slightly different point on the horizon. Professor Ray noted that today it is not until four or five minutes after the sun has emerged above the horizon that its rays start to penetrate the chamber, whereas five thousand years ago the alignment was presumably perfect, so that the chamber caught the very first dawn beams.

The likelihood of this phenomenon being purely coincidental is so minimal that we must accept that the orientation of the passage towards the point on the horizon where the sun rises at the winter solstice was part of the plan from the very beginning. Many have developed this notion to claim that Newgrange was designed as a temple and astronomical observatory rather than as a tomb. But because over sixty burials were discovered in P.J. Hartnett's excavation in the side-chambers of the Passage Grave at Fourknocks, close to the southern border of County Meath, and because you would hardly need such an elaborate structure to make an observation as to the falling of the shortest day, it seems unreasonable to claim that Newgrange was not a tomb. Although the temple theorists dismiss the presence of human bone in Passage Graves like Newgrange as irrelevant to the purpose of the mound, the great majority of people are happy to accept Newgrange's funerary role.

As mentioned earlier, there are resemblances between Newgrange and the Pyramids of Egypt. If we take the usually accepted date of around 3200 BC for the building of Newgrange, we realise that it is the senior monument, probably a few centuries older than its remote cousins on the Nile.

The fact that the burial chamber in Newgrange today is as dry as a bone, with no water percolating through the roof from the mound above, is a great compliment to the skills of the Newgrange builders; not only were they astronomers with a keen eye for the movement of the celestial bodies, they were engineers of a high calibre. Even the job of moving stones that weighed many tons into position to create the chamber ceiling must be considered a remarkable achievement, and there are subtleties undreamt-of until Professor O'Kelly took off the mound-covering above the passage and chamber. On the upper surfaces of their roof-stones, he noticed a continuous channel or groove that obviously had been created to drain away any water that might otherwise get into the chamber. Furthermore, if you look at those stones of the burial chamber which are laid in roughly circular form (in the so-called corbel technique), you will observe that the stones are not horizontal but tilted slightly upwards towards the centre of the chamber, the intention being, again, to prevent moisture percolating downwards into the chamber.

The Newgrange tomb is of the same cruciform design as Dowth North and Knowth East, with niches leading off to right and left of the central chamber as well as straight ahead. Here again the most lavish decoration is reserved for the right-hand niche, where the capstone is covered with a variety of motifs, some of which disappear in behind the wall, suggesting that it was carved before being placed in position. Beneath it is a fine pocked and modelled basin, with two concave depressions which may well have been used for the deposition of the cremated bones of the dead, although no one can be sure at this remove in time.

Fig. 81: The triple spiral carved on a wall of the hindmost recess in the Newgrange tomb has become a 'logo' well known far beyond the bounds of the Boyne Valley.

The right-hand wall of the hindmost recess has a beautifully executed triple-spiral (fig. 81) which is, if anything, the international 'logo' of Newgrange, as it appears also on the massive kerbstone (see fig. 80, page 116) outside the entrance to the passage. This is one of the most expertly carved kerbstones of any Passage Grave in Ireland, with the triple-spiral on the left of a central vertical groove indicating, as at Knowth, the entrance to the tomb. To the right are further spirals, and interwoven with them in the design are a number of lozenge- or diamond-shaped motifs. On the bottom right there are designs that always remind me of bushy eyebrows.

This brings us to the tricky question of what Passage Grave art is all about. Those who executed it would scarcely have seen it as 'art' in our modern sense; it must have had some other purpose or function, probably associated with whatever ritual was carried on inside and outside the tomb. Dronfield has suggested that the designs may have been conceived under the influence of alcohol or drugs, to which many primitive peoples are allegedly addicted; but that still hardly helps explain the significance of the motifs. Various explanations for individual patterns have been suggested on the basis of ethnographical parallels; even so, the truth of the matter is that we will just have to continue guessing what they meant to the contemporaries of those who carved them.

The very fact that a few of the stones do seem to show a very stylised version of the human face or figure could lead us to the conclusion that many of the designs could be good or bad imitations and stylisations of more easily comprehensible geometrical motifs, such as spirals, circles, triangles, zigzags, etc. But, if so, what originals were being imitated or stylised? On what could such patterns have been earlier used for them to have been copied in stone on the walls of Newgrange and other tombs in the Boyne Valley? O'Kelly wisely dubbed Newgrange 'a house of the dead' – in other words, a place where the dead could feel comfortable and be provided with a 'home from home'. Not a single piece of wood survives from any of the Irish Stone Age houses that we know of, so that it is impossible to establish if some of these patterns were carved originally in the much more malleable medium of wood. Ethnographic parallels among faraway peoples – in the Americas, for instance – show that they have colourful, geometrically designed motifs decorating their fabrics, whether for clothing or for tapestries, and it could be suggested that woven designs were the source for some of the Passage Grave markings.

Perhaps it is better to be kept guessing, so that we all have something to talk about!

No definitive answer can be provided either, of course, to the question of why such elaborate planning and vast effort over a number of years went into providing the opportunity for the sun to shine into the dark recesses of a chambered tomb for a mere seventeen minutes on four or five days of the year. Attempting to explain the structure as an observatory begs a further question, since all that trouble would not have been necessary just to fix the point on the horizon where the midwinter sun rose. No, there must also have been a magic involved in seeing the sunshine creep stealthily across the chamber floor only to disappear as silently as it had come – a magic which must surely have likewise struck O'Kelly when he encountered it a mere three decades or so ago. And the magic may have been the message. Here was a truth being imparted both to the dead, inside, and to the living, who penetrated the chamber from the outside at the winter solstice. Surely the point was being put across that, in the same way as midwinter is nature's nadir, after which the crops and trees begin to blossom and bud, so also death is not an end of human life, but a new beginning. In other words, this must be a testimony to a belief in an afterlife.

The importance of the sun for the Newgrange monument – and, at different times of year, probably also for other Irish Passage Graves, particularly those in County Meath – must surely be related to the god these people worshipped. As they were either an illiterate folk or one whose symbolic language, as used in their carvings (fig. 82), we can no longer understand, it is very difficult for us to know much if anything of any religion they might have practised, but the importance of the sun in the whole planning of Newgrange must surely make it the prime candidate to have been their major deity.

Whether there is another passage and chamber contained within the massive Newgrange mound remains to be seen. There could perhaps be one directed at the sunset on some other important seasonal date, but Professor O'Kelly, despite his best efforts, could find none. The mound manages to keep its secret still. For its very mysteriousness, for the feeling of communicating across the centuries with these highly intelligent, artistic people,

119

Fig. 82: Around the back of the Newgrange mound is this stone remarkably decorated with spirals, net-like weaves and other motifs, as shown here in a photograph taken during excavations some thirty years ago.

Newgrange will always manage to cast a spell, to fascinate and set the mind abuzz with a thousand unanswered – and unanswerable – questions. It takes us back to the beginnings of Irish civilisation, not Celtic but long pre-Celtic, which set the standard for later generations of artists and craftsmen in implanting in the Irish a love of geometric and stylised ornament. The Bend of the Boyne Passage Graves were (and are) something special, and they created in this one small area that feeling for a sacred landscape which was to command respect for many centuries after Newgrange, Knowth and Dowth had been abandoned as places of burial, sometime after 2500 BC.

Sacred landscape

The very fact that there was not just one great mound in the Bend of the Boyne but three shows just how important this area had become by the time the tombs came to be built in the period around 3000 BC. Perhaps there had already been a developing regard for this area as a particularly hallowed terrain by the time the earlier Neolithic house at Knowth was built over by the great tomb. Indeed, one might well ask whether some pre-tomb structures, such as the sub-rectangular house discovered by George Eogan at Knowth, could have been more than just dwellings but some kind of temple or at least religious house for the celebration of an unknown ritual. And what function was fulfilled by the palisade trench that likewise preceded the building of the main mound?

Certainly, after the heyday of the Bend of the Boyne tombs, which was probably winding down by the middle of the third millennium BC, the area of the lower Boyne Valley continued to attract its ritual devotees, peoples who may in part have come from outside the country and who used different kinds of pottery – the so-called Grooved Ware, associated with some henge monuments in England, and Beaker Ware, often associated with the introduction of metallurgy into Ireland around the second half of the third pre-Christian millennium. Nevertheless, the old Passage Grave builders did not just disappear; they would seem to have played a part in some of the Late Neolithic/Copper Age ritual structures that are usually to be found clustered around the major Passage Grave sites.

One example, some distance away from the main grouping, is Monknewtown, situated close to the Mattock River, which drains into the Boyne near Oldbridge. Here David

Fig. 83: In 1775, Gabriel Beranger portrayed men measuring large stones that once formed part of a major megalithic monument at Cloghlea, near Dowth, but which have long since disappeared. Our only visual record of it, Beranger's drawing is preserved on page 13 of the Royal Irish Academy's manuscript 3.C.32.

121

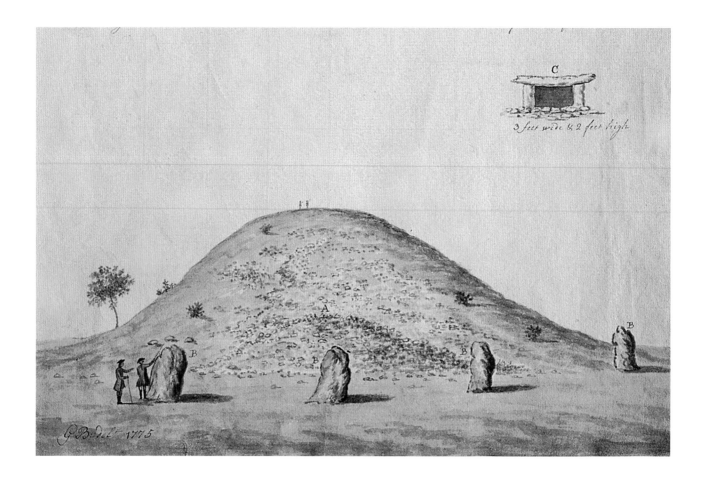

Fig. 84: The ring of large stones placed around the Newgrange mound roughly a thousand years after it was built are brought out clearly in this view of the Passage Grave painted when Gabriel Beranger did a tour of the Boyne Valley in 1775. It is now preserved on page 4 of the Royal Irish Academy's manuscript 3.C.30.

Sweetman found remains of an embanked circular enclosure around 30 m in diameter; the earth had been scooped up from the interior to create the bank, which, having no ditch outside it, is unlikely ever to have had any defensive function, but instead was more probably constructed for the purpose of defining and enclosing a sacred area. Inside, some burials were found in pits, and one of these was accompanied by a bowl of Carrowkeel Ware – the pottery so typical of the Passage Grave people.

A far better-preserved example, and almost double the size of Monknewtown, is in a field to the east of Dowth. The importance of this structure is indicated by the fact that its earthen bank is over 18.4 m wide at the bottom and rises to a height of 4.6 m. Not very far away were once a number of impressive-looking standing stones; these were swept away during the nineteenth century, but have been preserved for us in a drawing by Gabriel Beranger (fig. 83, page 121).

Newgrange, more than any of the other Bend of the Boyne Passage Graves, seems to have become the focus of a number of ritual monuments. Anyone standing outside the great mound and looking down towards the Boyne cannot fail to notice a sizeable tumulus on the flood-plain close to the bank of the river. Though unexcavated, this is doubtless also a Passage Tomb, but it needs an aerial camera to realise that it is sitting inside yet another embanked enclosure, further cementing the cultural/ritual link between Passage Grave and embanked enclosure. There is a further example of such an enclosure, though minus any visible Passage Grave, not far away to the east; it too is more visible from the air.

At Newgrange itself, the visitor will notice that the great mound is partially surrounded by massive upright stones (fig. 84), of which twelve survive out of a probable original number of thirty-five that likely formed a ring with a diameter of about 90 m. These stones are undecorated and chunky, and for many years they were thought to have been an integral part of the main tomb. But excavation has suggested that the circle was constructed as much as a thousand years after the main mound.

A further massive monument at Newgrange was constructed after the large tomb but before the ring of large stones encircling it. To comprehend this monument it is easiest if you stand in front of the main mound, looking towards the entrance, and then glance to the right. You will see a whole series of low, oblong concrete posts which seem out of place in a field full of stones. These posts indicate the former locations of the pits and postholes of a Beaker-period henge monument. Henges were circular ritual enclosures; they were not necessarily of stone and did not necessarily have trilithons across the top, as Stonehenge does. This one can be seen as a wooden version, consisting of a circle with a diameter of about 110 m with a wooden palisade made up of one or more circles of stakes, without an exterior earthen bank but with cremation pits inside it. David Sweetman, who excavated a part of this pit circle, uncovered another one to the west of the great mound. Not to be left out, Knowth, too, produced an example of a pit circle.

Newgrange delivered yet one more surprise just a few years ago when a geophysical survey revealed traces of a pathway 9 m wide and some 70 m long to the east of the mound, which Victor Buckley described as 'an avenue of the dead' leading not to the main tomb but to another one that was probably destroyed in the nineteenth century.

In the next field to the east from the main mound you can just make out a curious monument like a vast inverted U, with the rounded end having its back to the Boyne and the open end facing roughly northwards. This is what is generally called a cursus. It comes up a slope from the north, and is closed off just over the top of the Newgrange ridge, where the henge monument and the small Passage Graves in the flood-plain come into sight. What exactly the purpose of such a monument was it is difficult to say, but it could have been the culmination of a processional way emanating from what may have been a ritual pond that has since dried up. It is perhaps best understood in the context of the Late Neolithic/Copper Age embanked enclosures and pit circles already mentioned. While there are a few other examples known, the only other famous cursus is on the Hill of Tara, where it has long been known as the Banqueting Hall.

Fig. 85: The Mound of the Hostages, a Stone Age Passage Grave dating from the latter half of the third millennium before Christ, is the oldest monument surviving above ground on the Hill of Tara.

The Hill of Tara

Though not strictly speaking in the Boyne Valley, the Hill of Tara should be seen as an adjunct to it, for it overlooks the river from a distance and fits comfortably into the valley's culture. Tara is not a hill that would nowadays make any great impression on the passing motorist, as it does not really seem high enough to be called a hill. Yet it is, at around 150 m, taller than most other places for miles around and, on a fine day, several counties are visible in the panorama its summit affords.

A gentle walk to its tallest point makes one realise why it has been chosen as a place of importance over thousands of years, starting with the Passage Grave people, who built here what is known as the Mound of the Hostages (fig. 85) sometime in the third millennium BC. This mound is a comparatively simple example, having no differentiation between passage and tomb, which is only 1.3 m across; apparently later than the great Boyne mounds, it differs from them in having been filled with secondary burials, accompanied by Bronze Age ceramics – food vessels, as well as cordoned and cinerary urns – which help fill out the funerary record in the Boyne Valley in the earlier part of the Bronze Age, down to about 1500 BC.

But, as the site of a Passage Grave, Tara also provided adjunct monuments related to those in the Bend of the Boyne. Prime among these is the cursus, generally known as the Banqueting Hall since the 1830s, when George Petrie tried to identify monuments on the hill which had been named in medieval literary sources. The twelfth-century compendium of Irish placename lore known as the *Dindshenchus* describes it as follows (when it had already been long abandoned):

> The ruins of this house are situated thus: the lower part to the north and the higher part to the south; and walls are raised about it to the east and to the west. The northern side of it is enclosed and small; the lie of it is north and south. It is in the form of a long house, with twelve doors upon it, or fourteen, seven to the west and seven to the east. It is said that here the Feis Teamhrach [Feast of Tara] was held, which seems true, because as many men would fit in it as would form the choice part of the men of Ireland. And this was the great house of a thousand soldiers.

The site may well have been used for banqueting in the earlier medieval period, but its similarity to the cursus at Newgrange would suggest that this earthwork dates back to prehistoric times and should be understood in conjunction with the surrounds of the Mound of the Hostages. Tradition says that 'all roads lead to Tara' and the Hall may indeed have been the culmination of a gathering of roads to form a ceremonial approach to what, even then, must have been one of the most important ritual sites in Ireland. One can imagine Stone or Bronze Age spectators lining the raised banks on either side to watch some stately procession entering the holy of holies.

Further pieces of a possible ritual jigsaw puzzle around Tara include a 'travelling earthwork' to the west, an embanked earthen enclosure at Ringlestown, not far away, and – even closer to Tara – a much larger one, known as Rath Maeve, due south of the Hill.

Like the trio of tombs on the Bend of the Boyne, Tara is on a raised ridge. Its earthworks are spread over a distance of two and a half kilometres. Some eighteenth-century antiquarians thought that, because the hill preserved no stone monuments but only rings and mounds of earth, Tara could not have fulfilled any of the heroic and historical roles

The Boyne Valley

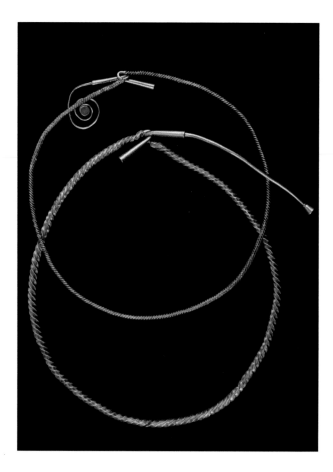

Fig. 86: The National Museum in Dublin preserves two large gold torcs found at Tara, suggesting that the site must have been an important place for ritual depositions in the period around 1200–1000 BC, long before the hill ever became the symbolic seat of the High Kings of Ireland.

which legend and literary sources have ascribed to it. Yet, since the beginning of the historical record in Ireland – going back to the seventh century – Tara has played an inordinately large role in this country, and its significance continued right down to the nineteenth century: Daniel O'Connell held one of the largest political rallies ever seen in Ireland here in 1843, bringing hundreds of thousands to hear him plead for a repeal of the Act of Union – without a megaphone in sight.

It was during the later prehistoric Iron Age that Tara – and the Bend of the Boyne – really began to come to the fore again, though two gold torcs of *c.* 1200–1000 BC, now in the National Museum (fig. 86), show that Tara was also important during the Bronze Age. It should be noted, too, that a number of almost imperceptible burial barrows on the hill may demonstrate greater habitation continuity here than has hitherto been assumed. One such barrow has been excavated; it was shown to contain five cremation burials, possibly of the early centuries ad and forming the first phase in the development of what is known as the Rath of the Synods, close to the churchyard on the hill. Only slightly later, it was transformed into a ring fort or *rath*, which gives it its name, consisting of four concentric banks and ditches; finds of a barrel lock and some glass suggest a connection with Roman Britain. This was at roughly the same time that Newgrange was apparently becoming a tourist attraction for overseas visitors; Romans from Britain were probably among those who came to admire that wonder of the ancient world, placing coins and gold coin-pendants (see fig. 51, page 76) in front of and near the entrance to the tomb. The earliest of these coins are from the reign of Domitian (AD 81–96), but the majority date from the third

126

and fourth centuries. The finding over the years of a total of 23 individual coins and a number of pieces of gold jewellery suggests that these may have been votive deposits, and that Newgrange was still a ritual magnet casting its spell far beyond the bounds of the Boyne Valley.

Roman coins of a different kind were found in the Rath of the Synods, but these would appear to have been placed there in the late nineteenth century as a sympathetic gesture by locals towards British Israelite excavators who had been disappointed in their hopes of finding the biblical Ark of the Covenant buried on the hill. As Mairead Carew has been discovering, the British Israelites were a body, including many Freemasons, who believed the British were one of the lost tribes of Israel and that the English language had been derived from Hebrew; their purpose was to demonstrate that the English were one of God's chosen people.

Mythologically Tara was alleged to have had its connections with the eastern Mediterranean, in that one folklore etymology for the name Tara associated it with the wall of a lady named Tea (*tea-múr*) who was the wife of Eirimón, a mythological King of Tara who – it is alleged – came from Thebes and is said to have died at Tara out of homesickness for his native Egypt. An alternative derivation, also offered by Cormac mac Cuilennáin, a king–bishop of Cashel around 900, was that the old Irish name for Tara, *Temair*, meant 'a lofty place' – which would fit in well with the panoramic view the Hill of Tara provides.

But back to the Rath of the Synods. This got its name because of a seventh-century Synod said to have been held there by Adamnan, Abbot of Iona. It was excavated half a century ago by Professor Seán P. O'Riordáin of University College, Dublin, whose findings have still to be published in detail. Over fifty years before his work, the British Israelites, even if they did not find the Ark, did at least discover that beneath a part of the site there

Fig. 87: Like cusped hands, the curving sides of Ráith na Ríg on the Hill of Tara enclose a pair of conjoined raths, the 'House of Cormac' and the Forradh, with the Mound of the Hostages beyond. The Rath of the Synods can be seen to the left of the church in the distance.

was a deep rock-cut ditch. The same feature was found in a cross-section of the bank and ditch of the Fort of the Kings (or Ráith na Ríg, to give it its correct Irish title). This is a hill-fort (fig. 87, page 127) that surrounds the whole top of the Hill of Tara like a necklet, with a diameter of about 250 m; the ditch inside its bank argues that it was not a defensive structure but a ritual demarcation of the enclosure that is the hilltop. In her recent excavation, Helen Roche found unexpected traces of metalworking activity in the ditch. At the centre of the hill-fort are two seemingly conjoined ring-forts known as Tech Cormaic and The Forradh. The latter, thought to have been the ancient royal seat, is a double-ramparted ring-fort with what may be house-foundations at its centre. The larger of the two is the House of Cormac, which has a raised centre that is now home to the Lia Fáil or the Stone of Destiny (see fig. 88, opposite), and is also the burial place of the insurgents who died in the Battle of Tara in the rebellious year of 1798.

The Cormac of 'House of Cormac' is Cormac mac Airt, a mythical King of Tara who is said to have reigned in the third century BC. He is one of the earliest royal figures associated with Tara – albeit by very much later medieval sources. These sources agree that Tara was the most important place in ancient Ireland, and that its kingship – though a matter of much debate – was of great significance in early Ireland. Such dynastic discussions do not bring us back to the Stone Age, which is when the Mound of the Hostages was constructed, nor necessarily even to the Bronze Age, when Tara probably became a venerable cemetery site with all those small barrows we have seen, many of which can be picked out only by aerial photography. But because a barrow was enclosed by both the Rath of the Synods and the House of Cormac, there is a suggestion that the Iron Age inhabitants of Tara wanted to legitimise themselves by encompassing within their own living enclosures the bones of earlier possessors of the hill. We can thus be fairly sure that the origins of Royal Tara go back into the prehistoric period, some centuries before the arrival of Christianity. A good case can be made to see its rulers as 'priest–kings', that is, political lords who also served as religious leaders.

Medieval accounts stress the otherworldly connections of Tara through its main god and goddess, Lug and Medhbh (or Maeve, after whom the henge known as Rath Maeve is named). Lug, the good god of the pagan Celts, was, it would appear, the divine manifestation of the Kingship of Tara, with Medhbh as the female aspect of the kingship, its fertility and, ultimately, the symbol of its sovereignty – as Tara's latest historian, Edel Bhreathnach, so neatly puts it.

Lug's arrival at Tara is described dramatically in the ninth-century *Battle of Moytura*. He comes unannounced to Tara, crowned as a king and dressed as a warrior, to beg admittance. The doorkeeper explains that no one can enter Tara without an art or a craft, and asks Lug what kind of artist (*aés dána*) he is. Lug says he is a wright, to which the doorkeeper replies that Tara already has one, and refuses him admittance. Then Lug says he is a smith, and is again refused entry because there is already a smith within the walls. Lug goes through a whole range of his talents, each time getting the same response. Finally he begs the doorkeeper to go and ask the king if Tara has anyone who combines *all* of these gifts; admitting defeat, the king has no option but to allow him in as master of all the arts (*samildánach*). Henceforth Lug is associated by all the people with the Kingdom of Tara, which is thereby invested with its own particular sacred character. An ancient list of Tara Kings says that one of its early royals, Conn of the Hundred Battles, was actually granted Tara by Lug.

One day Conn mounted the ramparts of Tara with his druids and *fili* (poet seers) to try to ensure that the people of the fairy mounds would not take Ireland unaware. As he was walking, he trod on a stone which screamed audibly all around Tara, the number of cries it uttered being the number of Conn's descendants who would be Kings of Tara. The stone was declared by the *fili* to be the Lia Fáil (fig. 88), the Stone of Destiny, said to cry out only when a good and real king entered Tara. It is equated with the penis-shaped pillar now placed upright in the House of Cormac but thought likely to have come originally from the Mound of the Hostages. This seems a most unlikely candidate for a stone that was trodden upon during a walk along the ramparts, though the alternative contender for the title – the upright stone, bearing the carving of a small figure, that stands beside the church – is only

Fig. 88: The Lia Fáil, or Stone of Destiny, on the Hill of Tara must have been a potent symbol for those visiting this hallowed site a thousand and more years ago.

129

marginally less unlikely, because flat. Whichever stone it was, the Lia Fáil was probably the inauguration stone of the Kings of Tara.

One of the symbols of the old pagan kingship of Tara was the holding on the site of a great feast known as the *Feis Temro* or *Teamhrach*, which seems to have been a fertility rite celebrating the divine nature of the King of Tara. It was held, suggests the *Dindsenchus*, in the great Banqueting Hall.

Cormac mac Airt – he of the 'House' on the Hill – is probably the most famous early King of Tara. The Irish Annals give his forty-year reign as falling in the third century after Christ, at the same time that Fionn mac Cumhaill and his Fianna warrior band were performing their legendary exploits. Cormac gained the kingship because he made a wise judgment about sheep where his predecessor made a bad one, as a result of which the latter's house fell down the slope at Tara – the folk explanation given for the so-called 'sloping trenches' at the northwestern end of the hill. Cormac was the classic good king, for sovereignty was seen in early Ireland as being associated with justice and with the fertility of land.

He is also the king traditionally associated with the Banqueting Hall beloved of medieval tales. Both *The Book of Leinster* and *The Yellow Book of Lecan* provide a plan of the hall around the king, where he would expect to have seated his smith, seer, judge, spearman, sureties, queen, hospitallers, leeches, leather-bottle makers, jesters, horn-blowers, charioteers, fishermen, flute-players, hunters, fishermen, trappers and fence-makers – all arranged in a tightly controlled pecking order according to their status. It was such festive occasions, when all sat down together, that inspired Thomas Moore's famous ballad of 1808:

> The harp that once through Tara's halls
> The soul of music shed
> Now hangs as mute on Tara's walls
> As if that soul were fled.
> So sleeps the pride of former days
> So glory's thrill is o'er
> And hearts that once beat high for praise
> Now feel that pulse no more.

Fig. 89: The nineteenth-century church on the Hill of Tara is now home to an audio-visual presentation that tells of the importance of this venerable ancient site down the centuries – and back into the mists of prehistory.

The king was expected to have particular regalia, as enumerated in an eighth-century tale about the race of Conaire Mór: a chariot and cloak of kingship; the two stones Blocc and Bluigne (probably called after two of the druids of Conn of the Hundred Battles), which were meant to open up before the rightful king; and Fál, the Stone of Destiny, crying out against his chariot-axle. He was hedged in by very ancient-sounding taboos: that he could not pass Tara on his right, nor stay away from it for more than nine days; neither could he spend the night in a house in which firelight was visible outside after sunset, and into which a person could see from outside – and a single man and woman together could not come into the house after sunset. One of the more curious taboos was that no plunder could be undertaken during his reign. Even more curious – for a monarch whose hallmark should be justice – is the diktat that he should not settle a quarrel between two of his subjects. Old Irish literature is garnished with tales of how particular kings were forced – as in a Greek tragedy – to break one taboo after another until they died. Cormac mac Airt had

to abdicate because he was blinded, as kings had to be physically perfect to rule (see page 76). The King of Tara also had his talismans that brought him luck: deer, bilberries, cress, water and hares from very specific places – and fish from the Boyne, famous even then!

Cormac mac Airt is said to have had associations with Connacht in his youth, and the people called the Uí Néill, who probably expanded from west of the Shannon before

Fig. 90: Evie Hone's 1936 stained-glass window in the former Protestant church at Tara represents The Descent of the Holy Spirit, *an appropriate theme that suffuses the sanctity of this ancient site that was pagan and Christian in turn.*

becoming masters of much of Ulster and the midlands, also came to claim the Kingship of Tara. It should be added, however, that there is a strong Leinster tradition that the Leinster kings were also once lords of Tara, and to them is also ascribed the building of Rath Maeve, the henge south of Tara. The founder of the Uí Néill dynasty, Niall Noígiallach – better known as Niall of the Nine Hostages – when dividing out lands among his many sons gave Tara to Lóegaire, who was the man in charge of Tara when St Patrick appeared on the scene (of which more below). Tara, at this stage, would appear to have been the residence of the king – at least for part of the time – and presumably remained the place of regal inauguration.

After Lóegaire's death in 461, the Connacht branch of the descendants of Conn of the Hundred Battles gave one king to Tara (Ailill Molt), after which the kingship reverted to the descendants of Niall of the Nine Hostages in both their branches, the northern and southern Uí Néill. It was one of the latter, Diarmait mac Cerbaill, who held the last pagan feast of Tara, around 560. He it was, too, who was involved in the cursing of Tara by St Ruadhán of Lorrha in County Tipperary. Ruadhán had given sanctuary to a Connacht prince who had murdered one of Diarmait's officials, so the king went to Lorrha, extracted the miscreant from his hiding place and had him brought to Tara to face execution. But Ruadhán, assisted by St Brendan of Birr, followed them to Tara. Here they fasted against the king – which is what you did in ancient Ireland if you wanted to get your way. However, the king fasted right back at them every night. Finally, the saints tricked the king into submission, and prophesied that the king's descendants would not rule over Tara, which would be abandoned.

Fiction or fact, the tale suggests that all subsequent Kings of Tara were Christian, and that henceforth 'King of Tara' was the title to be adopted by anyone who would achieve the high-kingship of the whole country. But while *The Annals of the Four Masters* dub many Kings of Tara as High Kings, the more conservative *Annals of Ulster* allow only eight names to bear the title King of Ireland in the six centuries from 600 to 1200. Of these, the first who could truly claim to have been *de facto* King of All Ireland was Máelsechnaill mac Máel Ruanaid (846–862); others – including Brian Boru – need not interest us here.

It is probably not unreasonable to claim that Tara was abandoned as a permanent or semi-permanent residence of the Uí Néill kings in the sixth century or not long afterwards, and that subsequently the title became more of a symbol, the kings residing where their own power-bases were located. Tara was left to become the grassed-over earthworks we see today, so that only in our imaginations can we see the wooden buildings that must once have stood there. The process of Christianisation and abandonment was summarised in the Prologue to the *Martyrology of Oengus*, written about 800:

> Tara's mighty burgh perished at the death of her mighty princes:
> With a multitude of venerable champions the great height of Armagh abides.
> Right valiant Lóegaire's pride has been quenched – great the anguish;
> Patrick's name, splendid, famous, this is on the increase.

In a word: The pagan king is dead, Long live Christianity. But even the 1822 Church of Ireland church (fig. 89, page 131) here has now been deconsecrated to allow it to be used for an audiovisual presentation – although *Pentecost* by Evie Hone (fig. 90), arguably one of the finest stained-glass windows in the extended valley of the Boyne, is still preserved within.

The Hill of Slane and the coming of Christianity

There are few places better than the Hill of Slane to get a majestic vista southwards over the plain of southern Meath (Brega) and beyond to the Dublin/Wicklow Hills, and on the other side over central Ulster to the Mourne Mountains. With one of the most impressive views offered anywhere along the Boyne, this hill rises to a height of just over 150 m. It is traditionally seen as the place where St Patrick started his showdown with the Tara King's druids and their paganism, told in theatrical detail in Muirchú's seventh-century *Life of St Patrick* and in even more dramatic language in the *Tripartite Life of St Patrick* some two centuries later – both accounts, of course, written hundreds of years after the alleged events, and both for propaganda reasons.

St Patrick had been up in County Down when Easter approached – in the year traditionally said to be 433. Inspired by God, says Muirchú, the saint and his followers decided to hold their first Irish Paschal celebration in the plain of Brega, where was 'the head of all paganism and idolatry'. So they set sail and landed at Inbher Colptha (see page 94) – the mouth of the Boyne – and went upriver to 'the burial Mounds of the men of Fiacc' – normally interpreted as Slane, although it has been justifiably argued that the Passage Graves on the Bend of the Boyne are meant. It is, perhaps, preferable to leave open the location of the event – particularly as we cannot even be sure it ever happened. By way of explanation, Muirchú adds that it was said these 'men of Fiacc' were the slaves had who dug the graves.

Anyhow, Patrick celebrated the Easter mass and lit the Paschal Fire. It was the custom of the pagan king to light a similar fire at the Feis Temro, the Feast of Tara, and, under pain of death, no one had the right to light such a fire other than the king. He was appalled to find someone else doing what was his right alone. His wizards warned him that unless the fire be quenched that same night, it would burn until Doomsday.

So the king had his horses harnessed to his chariot, and charged off with his entourage to where Patrick was – even though his magicians had advised him to stay away from this impostor, whom they said they would deal with themselves. The saint was summoned to where the king's people were; only one rose in reverence at his coming, and that was Erc, who was to become the patron saint of Slane (see page 66). The wizard Lochru immediately started to denounce the Trinity and the new faith of Patrick who, by return, requested that the Lord raise up this noisome necromancer and let him die – which, of course, transpired.

The king waxed mighty wrath and wanted to kill the saint, who called down darkness over the plain and caused a great earthquake and trembling of arms. It seemed to the king's men that the sky fell on the earth, and the horses bolted in fright, and the wind hurled the chariots through the fields. The king then invited Patrick to a contest with his druids at Tara.

The next day Patrick appeared in the midst of the king's men, though the doors were closed. One of the druids put a drop of poison into Patrick's drink but, after the saint had blessed the vessel, its liquor content curdled so that, when he turned the vessel upside-down, the drop of poison alone fell out. One up to Patrick. Then the druids decided to have a contest of miracles. They called down snow to the height of a man's belt on the plain of Brega, but when Patrick challenged them to get rid of it they could not do so immediately; whereas he himself was instantly able to melt it. Two-nil to Patrick. Then they succeeded in calling for darkness to descend upon the plain, but, equally, could not dispel it until the following day. Once more Patrick did the trick, so the score was three-nil. Various other contests took place in which Patrick was each time victorious, eventually winning (to switch

Fig. 91: The Franciscan friary on the Hill of Slane, shown here in a late-eighteenth-century watercolour by Thomas Malton, provides a wide panoramic view over parts of the Boyne Valley.

our sports!) game, set and match. The king himself was only half-convinced by all of this, but he allowed his subjects to become Christian.

Many pinches of salt are needed to accept all or any of this story, of course. References in the text to Egypt and Babylon, and the resemblance of Patrick's sudden appearance to that of Christ after the Resurrection, lead to speculation that the whole account is the figment of a fertile imagination building upon biblical sources. But its abiding message is that the Paschal Fire St Patrick created by the Boyne is a symbol for his bringing the light of Christianity to Ireland, fulfilling the fear of the druids that the fire would burn until Doomsday. Fifteen hundred years later, it still does.

On the whole there are no physical remains from St Patrick's time. Most of the extant buildings belong to the sixteenth century (*fig. 91*), and are discussed briefly elsewhere (see page 67).

Fig. 92: The baptismal font of c. 1500 that features angels and a bishop (as well as biblical scenes not shown here) was moved in 1991 from the former Protestant church in Clonard to its present position behind the altar of the Catholic church in the village.

Upstream to Clonard

Before going to Tara, St Patrick had – according to the *Tripartite Life* – left his disciple Lomman, a Briton, to guard his boat at the mouth of the Boyne. But, after the pagan King Lóegaire had been vanquished, the saint ordered Lomman to go to Trim, where Lóegaire's son Feidlimid lived. Feidlimid was quickly converted, along with his family, and St Patrick, arriving shortly afterwards, was delighted to see that someone of such eminence had been gained so easily for God.

Let us now proceed upstream beyond Trim as far as Clonard, where we are introduced to an important monastic chapter in the Boyne's history.

St Patrick's ecclesiastical organisation was presumably based on what he knew from Britain, where a church would be founded in any population centre that had sufficient numbers to support it. But Ireland did not have the system of towns so ubiquitous in Roman Britain; instead it had rural 'palaces' for the 150 or so regional kings, and these would probably have had only a small regal retinue within their walls. This was a system not suited to having newly established churches grafted onto it, and thus many of St Patrick's foundations did not prosper after his death. But the gaps left on his demise were filled within decades by a new phenomenon: monasticism. This was a movement encouraging personal spirituality within the framework of people of the same sex living together in a community and giving praise to the Lord. The movement had become popular in the lands bordering the Mediterranean, and it seems to have struck just the right note among the Irish, who in considerable numbers readily embraced the new way of life. It seems possible that Patrick may have encountered monasticism on his travels and personally encouraged its growth in Ireland, but it was not until the early decades of the sixth century that the idea seems really to have taken root, monasteries beginning to spring up like daisies across the green fields of an Ireland that had become holy.

Even if it was not the first of these, Clonard, near the upper reaches of the Boyne, has the reputation of having been one of the greatest, and a most notable 'nursery of saints'. The monastery's story was written by Elizabeth Hickey as *Clonard: The Story of an Early Irish Monastery, 520–1202* (1998) only a few years before her death.

The monastery was started by St Finnian, a Leinsterman, around 520. By this time the men of Leinster had had to cede their claim to the lands hereabouts to the men of Meath, but even so Finnian, arriving here after his travels to Wales and to Tours in western France, was made welcome. He was presumably given land close to the Boyne to settle down and found his monastery. He must have been a man of considerable charisma, for he had soon surrounded himself with a galaxy of men who themselves were to go out and found monasteries; they included the Ciaráns of Seirkieran and Clonmacnoise, the Brendans of Birr and Clonfert, Colmcille or Columba of Iona, and Ruadhán of Lorrha. Is it any wonder, then, that Finnian won for himself the sobriquet 'Master of the Saints of Ireland'? Although the number is certainly an exaggeration, three thousand student saints are said to have sat at his feet, and were not let leave without a book or a crozier or some other sign of the religious instruction they had received there.

In time, the monastery gained a great reputation for scholarship. Ailerán the Wise, one of the best-known members of the community in the seventh century, was celebrated for his knowledge of Greek, among other things. The old Irish Annals list the names of numerous later abbots, and indicate that the monastery continued into the second millennium. Although we hear of a cross, a church and a Round Tower having been there, it is sad to record, for a monastery of this importance and renown, that not a stone remains upon a stone of this venerable establishment at Clonard. Not even the abandoned Protestant church would appear to retain a trace of any pre-Norman ecclesiastical structure. The only significant remnant of medieval Clonard – though produced doubtless long after the monastery itself had closed down – is an attractive carved baptismal font (fig. 92) of *c.* 1500, which is now behind the altar of the Catholic church in the centre of the village. It has carvings of angels and a bishop/abbot (St Finnian?), together with a charming representation of the Flight into Egypt, with the Virgin and Child on the donkey in one panel and Joseph (identifiable by his carpenter's T-square) in the adjoining one, as he brings his family to safety in Egypt. Predictably, they are joined by a carving of Christ being baptised in the Jordan.

By comparison with the rest of Ireland, the number of early medieval monasteries in the Boyne Valley appears not to have been great, and it is one of the features of the valley that there are scarcely any surviving churches which can be reliably ascribed to the period before the Cistercians came to Mellifont in 1142. The century leading up to that event was one when the Romanesque style of building and decoration was very much in vogue throughout much of Europe, yet today the Boyne Valley is almost entirely devoid of churches bearing any of the characteristic Romanesque decorative patterns on doors or chancel arches. One of the few obvious exceptions is at Duleek, which is on the Nanny rather than the Boyne, and which had only a single Romanesque head capital, dating from about the third quarter of the twelfth century, that is no longer visible on the site.

This paucity of pre-Cistercian churches, Romanesque or otherwise, comes as something of a surprise, bearing in mind that the landscape is so fertile and rich. One possible explanation is of course that such churches simply were not lucky enough to survive the ravages of time – yet this seems unlikely, as at least fragments of decorated stonework should still be extant. Another and perhaps more likely explanation is that the local practice may have been to build in wood, and no early wooden churches anywhere in the land have managed to endure the vagaries of a thousand years of Irish weather. Further, the sizes of the churches would almost certainly have been considerably smaller than that of a normal church today. To ascribe the absence of pre-Cistercian churches to an inability of the men of the Boyne counties of Kildare, Meath and Louth to build stone churches before the arrival of the Cistercians is absurd; such a notion is confounded by the existence of a number of Round Towers (see pages 149–152) that show a mastery of exalted building techniques. Similarly, the absence of Romanesque carving on Boyne Valley churches is not for lack of a tradition of stone sculpture there, for the quality of the valley's carved High Crosses shows that it can hold its head high in any European context.

It is to these High Crosses that we shall now turn in some detail.

High Crosses

The High Crosses that survive from the Boyne Valley – from places like Slane, Fennor and Colpe (the Colphtha where St Patrick landed at the mouth of the Boyne), and probably Donaghmore – are largely in the form of fragments. The same, it should be said, goes for some others found in counties Louth and Meath, with fragmentary crosses from Balsitric, Dulane, Girley, Killary and Knock. But outside the valley proper there are fine crosses virtually complete, singly or in groups, at Castlekeeran in County Meath, Termonfeckin in County Louth, and of course Kells in County Meath, which has one of the most significant collections of such monuments to survive anywhere in the country. Kells lies outside our chosen area, being on what is the Boyne's most important tributary, the Blackwater, but within our defined region we have one very important group of crosses at Monasterboice and another small cluster at Duleek (included here for convenience although, in fact, it is on the parallel river, the Nanny).

Duleek, an ancient Irish monastic site, we have encountered before (see page 77), albeit briefly; it was here that St Patrick left his stonemason, Cianán, to build a church, though few would agree with the notion that any surviving church in Duleek goes back to his time. In the nave of the ruined medieval church at Duleek there is the head of an unfinished cross. One face (see fig. 52, page 77), looking towards the west, bears a Crucifixion scene showing Christ in a loincloth and with exhaustively long, emaciated arms, accompanied by Stephaton, who offers him hyssop in a chalice placed perilously at the top of a pole, and Longinus, who pierces Christ's left side with his lance. At the junction of cross and circle there are raised discs decorated with interlaces of four quadrants. The other face merely has raised discs, flattened but uncarved, and this is true also of the whole central surface of the cross-head. This cross can probably be ascribed to the ninth century, and the same applies to the more complete cross on the north side of the former Church of Ireland church. This latter lacks only its cap and, though smaller than most of the complete High Crosses, shows a high degree of sophistication in its carving, conforming to the old adage that 'small is beautiful'.

This Duleek cross (fig. 93) shares a characteristic with only a few others of its kind: one face bears biblical figure sculpture and the other purely geometrical ornament. The centre of the east face of its head has seven bosses sitting in a circle like a nest of eggs; these were carved originally with spiral ornament, of which some traces seem to survive. Interspersed between these larger bosses are smaller peripheral ones that most probably imitate nail-heads. These let us into the secret that this side of the cross was almost certainly copied from a wooden cross, onto the centre of which a round disc of bronze (or possibly even wood) would have been hammered; the domed nail-heads were copied detail for detail by the sculptor when he reproduced it in stone, probably at a larger scale. On this hypothetical wooden cross it is quite possible that the other geometrical designs were carved into the wood, dividing up the whole surface of the cross-face into a number of neat panels. Some of the panels, such as those on the arm-ends and the bottom of the shaft, bear interlace, whereas the middle panel of the shaft and that forming the uppermost limb have fretwork designs, with meander patterns on the constrictions of the arms. The most unusual motif is the one at the top of the shaft, which represents a tree whose branches curl out into spirals which seem to end in what look like animal heads. This is no apple tree with a serpent tempting Eve to take its fruit but, more likely, a variation on the Tree of Life theme. It reminds us that, even if we don't know precisely why these patterns on the panels were

Fig. 93: The High Cross at Duleek is one of the smallest of its kind, but shows considerable quality in the carving of religious scenes and decorative panels on its faces and sides.

Fig. 94: The south side of the High Cross at Duleek features a menagerie of fabulous animals.

chosen, they almost certainly had a religious symbolism very clear to people looking at them when they were freshly carved, even though the significance is lost on us.

The same holds true for the fascinating menagerie carved on the narrow sides of the cross. Here we find fabulous animals on the upper surfaces, creatures which are not a product of the Celtic imagination that enliven the pages of *The Book of Kells* but a heritage of classical antiquity that has managed to reach as far north as Ireland through channels we have not yet been able to identify. The clearest figure of all is on the end of the south arm (fig. 94): a proud and splendidly haughty winged griffin, a product of oriental imagination combining the body of a lion with the head and wings of a bird. Here the griffin probably has a religious meaning, because early Christians equated Christ with the lion, as Lord of the Earth, and with the eagle, as Lord of the Skies; the two together thus symbolised his being the Lord of the Universe.

A winged lion, seen holding a book on the top of the shaft above the griffin, has sometimes been interpreted as a symbol of the evangelist Mark, though proof is lacking.

140

The corresponding figure at the top of the other side – a figure (possibly winged?) holding a book – has been interpreted as the evangelist Matthew but, if this interpretation be correct, where then are the other two evangelist symbols that we would expect?

The end of the north arm has another classical figure, again winged, and holding something indefinable in its front paws. Further curious animals are found in the uppermost panel on the sides of the cross, but no visit to the zoo would be adequate to confirm their precise zoological species.

The west face of the Duleek cross (see fig. 93, page 139) has a Crucifixion at its centre, with Christ portrayed in a manner similar to that on the same site's cross-head, described above. The series of three panels on the shaft is among the most puzzling on any of the High Crosses. The lowermost one depicts on the left a figure, probably female, holding a child, with a second figure on the right holding up something that has an irregular round shape. The Holy Family would be an obvious subject, but the details do not fit any of the normal iconographies of Jesus, Mary and Joseph. Another appropriate possibility is that this is a scene from *The Early Life of the Virgin*, a tale belonging to the apocryphal material of the New Testament which we know to have been widespread in Ireland. The two scenes above this one would fit better into the apocryphal tale than anything we know from the Bible proper concerning the Holy Family; these two panels would, in this scenario, represent the Virgin having bread brought to her in the Temple by an angel and, at the top of the shaft, her aged parents Joachim and Anne greeting one another at the Golden Gate. But who the other figures are on the head of the cross remains a mystery – though the two on the top of the cross, one holding a crozier, could well represent the Egyptian hermits Paul and Anthony who, in a sense, could be regarded as the founders of monasticism.

We meet Paul and Anthony again at Monasterboice, in County Louth. Monasterboice lies a few miles north of Drogheda, and is traditionally thought to have been founded by St Buite, who is said to have died on the same night that St Colmcille or Columba was born (521) – already presaging a link between the two establishments in the style, content and richness of their High Crosses. Helen M. Roe, who wrote the charming book *Monasterboice and its Monuments* (1981), made us aware that the monastery preserved a relic of the head of its founding saint until this was stolen in 1521, becoming the subject of a slanderous court case, after which it disappeared and was never heard of again.

The monastery itself emerges into the light of actual history in the eighth century, after which it is known to have been a centre of learning, exemplified by its lay teacher Flann Mainistrech (*fl.*1056), who compiled a famous Synchronism of the Kings of Ireland and Scotland from the time of Lóegaire in the fifth century, and wrote poems to make it easier for his students to learn about the earlier history of Ireland. The monastery was certainly extensive in the tenth century, when it was attacked by Domnall, King of Ireland, causing the death of 350 people all in one house.

The old Irish Annals list the names of a number of abbots of Monasterboice, including two named Muiredach – one who died in 844 and the other in 924, the latter having apparently been the more important of the two. The name Muiredach found on one of the High Crosses is normally associated with the later abbot, but may not be that of either of them, for abbots are not the only people to have had their names inscribed on High Crosses. The Muiredach who, the inscription tells us, had the cross erected could equally well have been a local king of that name, so we would be well advised not to be too rigid about dating the cross on the basis of identifying Muiredach with one or other of the abbots

Fig. 95: The original crispness of the carving on Ireland's High Crosses can be surmised by looking at the underside of the arm and ring of Muiredach's Cross at Monasterboice where wind and rain have had far less weathering effect than on other surfaces of the cross.

of that name. From the iconographical point of view, a date in between the two abbots – around the second half of the ninth century, say – would probably be more appropriate not just for Muiredach's Cross but also for the other great cross at Monasterboice.

This Cross of Muiredach is the first one that we encounter on entering the churchyard (which occupies a part of the old monastic site). It is a solid, stocky ring-headed cross consisting of three pieces: base, cross, and capstone on top. It bears more individual figures than any other Irish High Cross, and these are carved in such a high false relief that the outline of their figures sometimes juts out beyond the framework of the cross, which is a rounded moulding going all the way around the edges and corners. The immediate impression is that of a well-ordered system of panels, not always based on the horizontal, and each carefully framed by a rope-like surround.

What we have here, as on the other Irish crosses, is a selection of scenes from the Old and the New Testaments (together with Saints Paul and Anthony), the intention of which is to present stories in a visually narrative form that can promote ideas and tenets of church doctrine to a public, lay or ecclesiastical, who, through contemplation of the individual scenes, would be led to a firmer Christian belief and to thoughts of piety and prayer. One could well imagine an early medieval monk explaining the contents of one or more scenes just as guides today interpret the biblical content of the crosses to tourists.

142

Because of the strongly bonded grains of the sandstone which makes up Muiredach's Cross, it is one of Ireland's best-preserved High Crosses. Anyone looking at the underside of the arm and ring (fig. 95) can get some idea of how beautifully crisp the original carving was, because these surfaces have not been exposed to the same degree of weathering as the main faces have been for a thousand years and more.

Leaving aside the bases, which have chariot and animal processions, and interlace, which cannot be interpreted satisfactorily, the cross displays a series of biblical subjects, starting with *Genesis* and ending with the Last Judgment at the centre of the east face of the head, and the Crucifixion, which occupies the same space on the other face of the cross.

As with so many of the Irish High Crosses, the series starts with Adam and Eve, our first parents, whose original sin necessitated that Christ would have to give his life on the cross to save mankind. On the lowermost panel on the east face we see Eve handing the apple to Adam (fig. 96) as the serpent crawls up the stem of the tree, whose apple-laden branches descend over the backs of the standing figures. Sharing the panel with them are their children Cain and Abel, Cain using a club to batter the head of his brother, whose death made him into the first innocent victim of the Old Testament, as Christ was to become the victim par excellence of the New. The panel above offers the classic configuration of Good versus Evil – the miniature figure of David standing in front of the seated Saul as the giant Goliath slumps to his knees, putting his hand up to his forehead to demonstrate that he has already been struck by David's slingstone. In the panel above we encounter Moses raising his stick to get water out of the rock in Horeb in order to ensure that the Israelites murmuring against him would not die of thirst on their desert path on the way back to the Promised Land. This is one of a number of scenes on the High Crosses designed to show how the Lord helped the faithful in times of danger – the so-called 'Help of God' theme.

Fig. 96: On the east face of Muiredach's Cross at Monasterboice, Adam and Eve share the lowermost panel with their offspring Cain and Abel, the latter of whom was a precursor of Christ as the first innocent victim of the Old Testament.

143

Fig. 97: The west face of Muiredach's Cross at Monasterboice, probably carved in the ninth century, invites us to reflect on the life, death, resurrection and ascension of Christ represented on it.

From there we suddenly jump to the New Testament, with a representation of the adoring Magi approaching the Virgin, who holds the Christ child diagonally across her lap – a rather rare compositional detail which we can trace back to an early-eighth-century fresco in Rome. We normally expect the Magi to number three, but here there is a fourth figure. Some have identified this as Joseph. However, as the four figures are similarly dressed, and because Joseph would not be shown presenting the child with a ring of gold, as the first of the four figures does here, there is a strong case to be made for seeing all four as Magi. Again Rome provides a precedent. As the Magi are considered to have come from the four corners of the earth, we can see an indication here of the Magi standing for the whole world in paying obeisance to the Christ child, who is appearing for the first time as a Theophany to his public adorers.

The head of the east face of the cross brings us to the most grandiose scene on any of the Irish Crosses, the Last Judgment – one of the earliest known representations of the theme to survive anywhere in Europe, and one which evokes both liveliness and a sense of humour among the more than forty figures which make up this wonderful composition.

Central to it is the figure of Christ, standing in an attitude like that of the Egyptian god Osiris, with a cross over one shoulder and a staff over the other, and with the eagle hovering above as a probable representation of the Resurrection. To Christ's left, as we look at the scene, is David the harpist; the Holy Spirit, in the form of a dove, whispers inspiration for the Psalms into David's ear while, behind him, we see the good souls, led by a flute-player and (probably) a singer reading from a book.

On the other side of Christ is one of David's musicians, with a triple-reeded flute and, across his lap, perhaps some other zither-like instrument. To his right is a devil with a three-pronged fork or trident, banishing all the bad souls to their eternal damnation – all, that is, except for the second figure from the end on the bottom row, whose head is turned towards Christ in the hope of reprieve . . . but in vain, for the pushing throng behind leaves him no option but to face the gates of Hell.

Beneath the Last Judgment is a scene often associated with it in medieval art, the Weighing of Souls, of which this is undoubtedly one of the oldest known examples. On the left is the Archangel Michael, traditionally seen as the one who will weigh us all when our time comes, and the small figure at Christ's knee in the scene above may be helping out by recording in his little book what judgment has been reached. In front of St Michael are the scales, with one pan empty and the other holding the soul whose deeds – to be imagined as being in the empty pan – are being weighed against him. But St Michael does not have the field all to himself. Beneath the scales is an impish devil, with intertwined legs, using a stick to push the empty pan upwards so that the soul in the other will fall down to him. The Archangel has discovered the deception in time and is ramming his own staff down the devil's throat – resulting, hopefully, in the fairy-tale ending that all except the baddy live happily ever after.

Christ is shown in Glory at the top of the Last Judgment scene, and the two figures above that may possibly represent Saints Paul and Anthony.

The other face of Muiredach's Cross, looking towards the west (fig. 97), has – as on most Irish crosses – the Crucifixion as its central theme (fig. 98). Above Christ's arms, two angels minister to him, while below we find Stephaton and Longinus delivering their hyssop and side-wound. On either side of Christ's knees are two knobs representing the sun and moon. Under Christ's right hand is a curious seated figure holding his legs up beneath his chin, while below Christ's left arm a further figure appears to clutch a baby – which helps to identify these figures respectively as Tellus, personification of the ocean, and Gaia, whose child represents the fertility of earth. When sun, moon, earth and ocean are all taken together, they are close enough to the fire, air, earth and water that were the elements of the ancient world to be regarded as making up the constituents of the cosmos. This can also be taken as the symbolic meaning of the ring encircling the cross (fig. 98), for the Crucifixion of Christ – which is at the centre of the circle – was seen by the early Christians as being the most central and, appropriately in this case, the most crucial event in the whole history of the cosmos.

The same cosmic theme can be seen to permeate the two lower panels of the shaft. The lowest (fig. 99, page 146), showing the Messiah flanked by two soldiers, is usually taken to represent the Arrest of Christ. But at his arrest Christ did not carry the staff or reed which is clearly shown here, and it is preferable to interpret this scene as Christ being mocked by soldiers as King of the Jews and thus King of the Earth, with his reed acting as his regal staff. The mantle over Christ's shoulder – the most decorative garment shown on any High Cross, fastened by what resembles a Tara Brooch – would then be the scarlet or purple cloak which the soldiers dressed him in as they taunted him as an earthly king.

The scene above is normally taken to show Doubting Thomas, the figure on the left as we see it seemingly putting his finger into Christ's right side. But this is scarcely acceptable,

Fig. 98: The Crucifixion of Christ is placed at the centre of the head of the west face of Muiredach's Cross at Monasterboice, surrounded by a ring which may have symbolised the cosmos for those who carved it a thousand years ago.

Fig. 99: The figure of Christ with decorative cloak being mocked as King of the Jews is represented on the bottom of the shaft of the west face of Muiredach's Cross at Monasterboice, which gets its name from that inscribed around the heads of the cats beneath.

because it is Christ's left side that is being pierced in the Crucifixion above. On the basis of parallels in the apses of early Christian churches in Rome, we would be more justified in seeing this panel as representing Christ raised up above the earth, blessing his disciples and telling them to go forth and teach all nations, and the two flanking figures as apostles, of whom Peter on the left places his hand close to Christ's side – but not into a wound. The curious blocks on which all three figures stand would support the notion that they are raised above the earth – i.e. that they are in the skies.

In representing Christ as Lord of the Earth and Lord of the Skies respectively, these two panels would seem to fit the cosmic symbolism of the four elements encircled in the ring above and of the Magi coming from the four corners of the earth in the Adoration scene on the east face of the cross-shaft. The topmost panel of the shaft, showing Christ handing a key to Peter and a gospel to Paul, also unites earth and Heaven in illustrating Christ's words to Peter: 'I will give unto thee the keys of the Kingdom of Heaven, and whatsoever you shall bind on earth shall be bound also in Heaven.'

The figures on the north arm of the cross are unclear – St Peter in the court of Caiaphas? – but the representation of the Resurrection on the corresponding south arm is unmistakable: Christ, flanked on each side by an angel, is wafted heavenwards above the tomb, which takes the shape of an inverted U and is guarded by kneeling soldiers. The panel on the top of the cross is probably the culminating scene of the Ascension, with the figure of Christ raising his arms and flanked by two figures, one of which at least can clearly be seen as an angel with wings. This scene is on the separate capstone, which has roof-shingles and the shape of a house or a church or a shrine – its precise significance has never been clarified.

The panel at the bottom of the shaft, interpreted here as the Mocking of Christ, helps shed light on one interesting point: the question of colour on the crosses. Not a trace of colour has ever been found on the Irish High Crosses, but surely the scene of the Mocking of Christ can only have had its full impact if Christ's cloak had been painted scarlet and/or purple, the colours named in the Gospels. We thus have a clue that the Irish High Crosses could originally have been painted, which would make them resemble the frescoes of Roman and other continental churches – with which the compositions of the biblical panels on the High Crosses have a lot in common, including the aim of inducing thoughts of piety and prayer among the faithful. Because Irish wooden churches of the time were probably both too small and too dark for paintings on their interior walls to be appropriate, we should perhaps see the High Crosses as Ireland's open-air answer to the continental frescoes. The similarity in the compositions of biblical scenes between frescoes and crosses may be due to both having common models – perhaps in the form of pattern books, which could have easily been transported from place to place.

The faces of the High Crosses did not have room for all the panels that needed illustration, and some further Passion pictures – Pilate washing his hands and perhaps another Mocking scene – had to be relegated to the arm-ends on the sides, where Saints Paul and Anthony are also found. But further signs of comic relief – yet presumably with a symbolic purpose as well – can be seen in the small vignettes at the bottom of the shaft: two men pulling each other's beards (perhaps representing discord), significantly on the north side (the direction from which in the medieval period evil was thought to come), and animals fighting or playing with one another on the other three sides. A detailed examination of this cross shows that the selection of scenes was very deliberate: they were carefully chosen to show the Help of God, the victory of Good over Evil and adversity, the prefiguration of New Testament scenes in those chosen from the Old, and the notion of Christ as King of the Earth and the Skies in a cosmic context.

By comparison, the reason for the choice of scenes on the other, taller, cross at Monasterboice, known as the West Cross (fig. 100, page 148), is somewhat more opaque, particularly as some of them are less easy to identify. On the east face we have a repetition of Moses striking water from the rock, joined by the Sacrifice of Isaac and by Samson

Toppling the Pillar of the Temple as examples of the Help of God. The chronological order is not followed on this face, with David and the Lion below and David with the Head of Goliath four panels up. Even the figure at the centre of the east face causes interpretational problems – it could be Christ, or David again – and the other panels on the head are no less difficult to identify, though the scene of the Three Children in the Fiery Furnace can be taken as certain at the bottom of the head, and Peter Being Saved from the Waters by Christ in a Boat near the top is extremely probable. The appearance of Peter is balanced on the other face by his presumed presence above the Crucifixion as he pulls his sword from its sheath preparatory to cutting off the ear of Malchus. Additionally, I would take the figure beside the crucified Christ's left hand, seen warming himself at a brazier as a cock crows above his arms, to be Peter in the court of Caiaphas. These figures of Peter are a measure of the importance which Rome played not only to the Irish Church but also as the ultimate source for the choice of biblical scenes on the Irish High Crosses.

The west face of the shaft of this West Cross at Monasterboice has a much-worn Christ in the Tomb panel at the bottom, surmounted by the Baptism of Christ, but the three-figure scenes above that are not adequately differentiated, nor their attributes delineated sufficiently clearly, to make any satisfactory identification.

The studs in the ring of this cross bear a certain resemblance to the enamel bosses on metalwork masterpieces such as the Tara Brooch and the Ardagh Chalice, plausibly demonstrating – as did the Duleek cross – that the great stone High Crosses are at least in part translations into stone of crosses made from other materials, such as wood decorated with bronze.

Though old Irish literary sources tell us little or nothing about High Crosses, other than giving us the title *ard chrois* ('High Cross'), one can at least say that this West Cross at Monasterboice lives up to its description: rising to a height of around 7 m, it is the tallest of all the High Crosses that survive from ancient Ireland.

Round Towers and the Vikings

These great crosses at Monasterboice stand in the shadow of a Round Tower (see fig. 100, opposite), one of the few surviving examples in the Boyne Valley area. This one is currently almost 26 m high, but even a cursory glance shows that it is incomplete; the lower part of the now totally vanished conical roof would have been at a level slightly higher than the present top, so that the original height was probably not much short of 30 m. In days gone by, a reconstruction in wood of the individual floors and interconnecting stairs allowed access to the parapet, but this is now no longer permitted because of possible hazard. Each floor is lit by a window, round or square-headed, or even pointed. Access to the tower was via a round-headed doorway almost 2 m above the ground – and it is this feature, typical of all but two of the known Round Towers, that has given rise to the age-old discussion about the purpose of these structures. Gone are the days when they were considered as Phoenician fire-towers or seen as pagan phallic symbols. As long ago as 1845 George Petrie showed that the towers had to be understood in the context of Christian monasteries, and that the old Irish name for a Round Tower was *cloigthech*, denoting a bell tower. But was it really necessary to have such a tall tower to ring a bell from? Of course, there are obvious parallels in the campaniles of Italy – from which the idea of the Irish Round Tower probably derived – and even in the Islamic minarets from which the muezzin call the faithful to prayer, but the question still remains.

Furthermore, why was the doorway usually so high above the ground? In the nineteenth century this feature gave rise to the notion that the towers had been erected as defences against the nasty Viking monk-bashers, the door being raised above the ground so that saintly defenders could climb up a ladder, pull it after them, close the door, and climb to the top of the tower to pour hot water or throw stones down on the Nordic marauders below. But then someone pointed out that the Irish were just as active at sacking monasteries as the Vikings; moreover, a flame-bearing arrow shot in through the window would cause the interior to blaze up very quickly, killing any monks inside.

Precisely such a fate overtook this tower at Monasterboice, for *The Annals of Ulster* reported in 1097 that *Cloictech Mainistrech* – the bell-tower of Monasterboice – was burned with its books and many treasures. The reference is valuable in telling us what was preserved in such towers. Mention of books need not be taken to suggest that this was necessarily the monastic library. We know that *The Book of Kells*, for instance, was considered as a relic of St Colmcille, so the books kept in Round Towers may also have been considered as relics, like the 'treasures', which were doubtless the reliquaries containing relics associated with the monastic founder and others – perhaps similar to those house-shaped shrines now preserved in the National Museum of Ireland, including some fragments of one from Clonard.

Perhaps the reason why the door was placed so high above the ground was to enable the monastic reliquaries to be displayed – but out of arm's reach of pilgrims; were pilgrims to be allowed to touch their contents there would soon be precious little left, much to the detriment of the coffers of the monastery, which would have regarded relics as a source of income from visiting pilgrims. The link with pilgrims might also help explain why the towers were so high, their distinctive cone-shaped tops being visible above the treetops like rockets heading for outer space: the sight of the tower from a distance would not only have given the approaching pilgrim a directional guide but would also have encouraged flagging spirits to keep walking until they got to their final goal.

Another valuable indication of the content of these Round Towers is found in the very first reference we have to one of them, a Boyne Valley example, now vanished, at Slane. *The Annals of Ulster* record that the Vikings of Dublin burned the bell-house here in 950, causing the death of a large number of people, including the monastery's lector, and the destruction of the founder's episcopal staff and 'the best of all bells' – again indicating that these towers constituted the monastic treasury, among other things. How long before the middle of the tenth century this particular tower had been built we cannot say, but by then the first great wave of Viking oppression was long over, so we need not see protection from the Norsemen as the prime reason for the construction of the towers. That said, the fact that the first reference to a Round Tower is to the destruction of one example need not exclude the possibility that such towers could have been constructed up to a century earlier, when the idea could have been borrowed from the Italian campanile at about the same time that, as we saw, Roman inspiration was contributing to the iconography of biblical scenes on the High Crosses at Monasterboice.

Fig. 101: Donaghmore, between Navan and Slane, is one of the oldest Christian sites in the Boyne Valley, with its almost perfect Round Tower standing out above the trees. Beside it is a belfry surviving from a late medieval church.

We know of other Boyne Valley monasteries that had Round Towers which have long since disappeared. Historical sources point to their former existence at Clonard, Ardbraccan (some five kilometres west of Navan) and Tullaghard (near Trim). But a very unusual proof of the former presence of such a tower is found at Duleek, on the Nanny. As is still visible at Lusk, in north Dublin, the Round Tower at Duleek had a square medieval tower built up against it. At some unknown time the old Round Tower crumbled and fell, leaving the negative impression of its former existence to be seen up to a height of about 12 m in the north side of the medieval tower.

In our chosen area of the Boyne Valley, there is only one Round Tower surviving in virtually perfect condition, and that is at Donaghmore (fig. 101), a few miles east of Navan. Its conical cap had collapsed by the late eighteenth century, but in 1841 the local landowner, Thomas Rothwell of Blackcastle, collected up all the pieces he could find and restored the tower to the form we see today. It is only marginally taller than the Monasterboice tower and, as there, its doorway is well above the ground. But the

Donaghmore doorway has one unique feature: the figure of the crucified Christ above it and a human head on either side. The crossed feet of the Christ figure are typical of the Gothic period, long after the presumed building period of the tower (before 1200), suggesting that at least the lower stone, on which the figure of Christ was carved, may be a later insertion, as indeed may one or both of the heads. The site was created by St Patrick for an otherwise unknown saint, Cruimthir Cassan, whose relics, it is said, were preserved here – perhaps even in the Round Tower. It is likely that a High Cross head now preserved in the National Museum also came from here.

Donaghmore and a number of other Boyne Valley monasteries with Round Towers were plundered by the Vikings, perhaps even before the towers were built, and we can imagine how the Viking ships rowed upriver striking terror into the hearts of the monks, burning their churches, stealing their reliquaries and doubtless carrying off many of the monks themselves as slaves. The Vikings made their first Irish settlement in County Louth, at what is now Annagassan, some miles north of the Boyne. That was in 840. Within a year they had founded a much more permanent settlement at Dublin, which was to become their most important Irish base for raiding and trading. Had they chosen instead to settle at the mouth of the Boyne, then Drogheda might well have become the capital of Ireland. Despite the sand-bar at the end of the estuary, the river's banks would have provided ample room for sailors to settle and a suitably sheltered anchorage where they could have pulled up their boats to load and unload both merchandise and human cargo. But such was not to be because, as John Bradley has cogently argued, the strong presence of the Uí Néill kings of Brega some miles upstream at Knowth would have discouraged any permanent Viking settlement, establishment of which might upset the political balance of power in the area.

During the second half of the first millennium AD, Knowth took on a whole new lease of life. It was made into a fortification through the digging of a defensive ditch just inside the old kerbstones of the mound and, at a somewhat later stage, a house (or houses) appears to have been built on top of the mound, which would not appear to have had a very strong defensive character.

Certainly by the ninth century, Knowth and the surrounding area had become the centre of the Kingdom of Northern Brega, ruled at first by a minor population group known as the Gailenga but, from about 800, taken over by the more important group called the Síl nAedo Sláine. These people had long given up realistic hope of ever becoming Kings of Tara, though it was geographically not far away from them, but during the ninth and tenth centuries they were able to keep their head high against competition from their Uí Néill cousins, the Clann Cholmáin, located farther west in the old Kingdom of Mide. On occasions, indeed, they were not averse to joining with the Norse invaders to maintain their power in the locality. The Vikings did not entirely leave them unscathed, however, as we know that Olaf, King of Dublin, destroyed the 'cave' at Knowth and the seat of the Kings of Southern Brega, at Lagore near Dunshaughlin, in a single week in 935.

By the eleventh century the power of the Knowth Kings was on the wane, though we do not know precisely when they finally abandoned their regal site. It is, however, interesting to note that, shortly after the coming of the Normans, Knowth was confirmed as being the property of the Cistercian Abbey of Mellifont; it may well have been owned by that monastery for years if not decades before this.

Mellifont

The foundation in the year 1142 of the Abbey of Mellifont (fig. 102) on the River Mattock, a tributary of the Boyne, heralded a whole new era of Irish monasticism. The abbey was different in many ways from the older type of Irish monasteries like Clonard, Duleek and Monasterboice. These had been independent spirits, each under the leadership of an abbot who was largely his own master; sometimes they combined with other monasteries to form a family grouping known as a *paruchia*, but as often as not they were unaffiliated to any other monastery – or even to any religious order (e.g. the Benedictines). They had mushroomed to fill an organisational gap in the decades after St Patrick's death and, as we have seen, had gained great popularity in subsequent centuries. In time, these monasteries became leaders in Bible studies, producers of manuscripts (if they were large enough to have their own scriptoria), and fosterers of arts and crafts, particularly in the making of reliquaries to house the relics of their founding saint. Through the annals they kept they were the invaluable recorders of history, and it is their codices which have preserved for us so much pagan lore. It might seem surprising to find such lore recorded in a Christian context, but the monasteries saw themselves as the custodians of old Irish culture and the literary forms which it had created down the centuries.

This did not mean, however, that these earlier Irish monasteries were the keepers of morals in our modern sense, or that the abbots were always pure as the driven snow. On the

Fig. 102: The abbey of Mellifont in County Louth, founded for the Cistercians in 1142, was heavily quarried for building stone in the earlier eighteenth century, leaving half of the lavabo (right) and the Chapter House in the centre, as seen in a 1793 engraving from Grose's Antiquities of Ireland. *The church on the left is a medieval parish church.*

contrary, the abbots were often laymen occupying a lucrative job – the medieval equivalent of manager of a modern business corporation, having many subordinates and with at least a concubine, if not one or more wives, lurking in the background. The sin of simony was not unknown to the leaders of Irish monasteries; 'jobs for the boys' practices and the Irish attitude to monastic celibacy did not meet with the approval of Rome, or of those who were watching over Rome's interests in these islands.

A movement towards church reform had been started in Rome during the course of the eleventh century by the great Pope Gregory VII, known as Hildebrand, whose name was given to the whole movement which swept across Europe within decades of his having received the obeisance of the German King and Holy Roman Emperor Henry IV at Canossa in 1077. Centuries earlier there had been an attempt to purge the Irish church of its impurities and go back to the strict rule of the sixth-century founders, combined with a greater observance of Holy Writ; this had been known as the Culdee movement, from the Irish name *Céle Dé*, meaning 'servants of God'. Though the Culdees kept up the struggle from the eighth until at least the tenth century, their efforts were thwarted by the laxer elements in the old Irish monasteries which quietly – and, one suspects, happily – went back to their familiar ways, if indeed they had ever abandoned them.

Fig. 103: Liam de Paor's excavations at Mellifont in the 1950s made possible the partial reconstruction of the old cloister arcade, seen here to the left of the lavabo, which itself is left of centre. The ruins on the right formed part of the kitchens and refectory of the monastery.

By the year 1100, then, the time was ripe for another wave of reform. This time it came from outside, emanating from Rome, which wanted to have all of Europe under its wing. St. Anselm, the Archbishop of Canterbury was displeased at what he saw on the western side of the Irish Sea, and he was one of those responsible in 1101 for getting what he took to be the High King of Ireland at the time, Muirchertach O'Brien, the King of Thomond, to call a Synod on the Rock of Cashel. The Archbishop and the prelates he gathered around him doubtless realised that it was unlikely they would succeed in reforming centuries of sinfulness (as they would have seen it) in a single sitting, but they made a start by trying to tackle simony, marriage within the forbidden degrees of kindred, and the Irish system of lay abbots.

By the time a new Synod returned to the fray at Rathbreasail a decade later, in 1111, the decision had been made to reorganise the church in Ireland. No longer were the old Irish monasteries to rule the roost, with a nonchalant disregard for the wishes of the Holy See. The papal legate, Gilbert, who was also the bishop of the Norse see of Limerick, prepared a thesis – probably best regarded as what we would today call a discussion document – in which he basically proposed that the power was to be taken from the old Irish monasteries and handed over to bishops, who were to rule over a new series of bishoprics which were, in many cases, co-terminous with political boundaries of the day. These in turn were to be subservient to two new archbishoprics, at Armagh and Cashel respectively, and ultimately to the Pope in Rome. This was all about – or almost all about – establishing the authority of the papacy over Ireland, and the easing out of the old Irish monasteries from the sphere of religious power. In time the reformers were to drain the lifeblood of the old Irish monasteries, many of which ceased to have any meaningful existence by the end of the twelfth century.

One of those who was to play a leading role in this Irish reform movement was Malachy O Morgair, who in time was to become Archbishop of Armagh and, years after his death in 1148, to be Ireland's first canonised saint. On his way to an intended visit to Rome in 1140, he visited two monasteries in France, one at Arrouaise under Augustinian rule and the other the Cistercian Abbey of Clairvaux in Burgundy. He was impressed by the religious life of the former, but was so overwhelmed by the personality and sanctity of the latter's abbot, Bernard, renowned for his preaching, that he requested permission from the Pope to join the Cistercian order so that he could spend the rest of his life there. Bernard obviously 'clicked' with Malachy too, to such an extent that – after Malachy's death – he wrote the Irishman's life, and requested to be buried beside him in front of the monastic high altar. However, the Pope refused Malachy's request, believing he would be of more use at home in Ireland. But at least Malachy was able to convince Bernard to allow some of his monks to come to Ireland to found what was to be the first of the country's many Cistercian monasteries – the great spearheads in the reform movement in Ireland. Here at Mellifont (fig. 103), on land granted by a local king, the Cistercians set up their monastery on the Mattock, introducing their strict monastic rule – a strong contrast with the lax communities which had been the norm in Ireland for centuries. Here, too, the continentals started introducing order into the sphere of monastic buildings.

The old Irish monasteries were not entirely as higgledy-piggledy in their layout as some people might like to imagine, but they frequently consisted of a number of small churches dotted around the monastic grounds without any too obvious plan, giving the impression that they just 'growed and growed' as the need arose. All of that was to change with the advent of the Cistercians. For a start, the scale was very different. Not even the monumentality of Cormac's Chapel, completed on the Rock of Cashel by 1134, could have prepared the Irish for the large size of the new Cistercian churches in comparison to their own – although anyone who had gone to Rome via France, or had seen the Cathedral in Durham in northern England, would have been far less surprised.

The Cistercians built their monasteries according to a preordained plan, one they were to use with only minor variations in monasteries built over many parts of Europe. At the heart of everything was, of course, the church – a long, tall structure with nave and aisles, subdivided by wooden partitions to keep priests and lay-brothers apart. The altar was in the choir, and the two transepts, north and south, had anything up to three chapels nestling on their eastern side. Usually to the south of the nave lay a grassy cloister garth, around which went a cloister – usually a lean-to structure where the monks could walk in silent prayer. Each side of the cloister-garth was adjoined by a building. To the north lay the church, while on the east was the sacristy (reached from the church) and a chapter room where the monks could congregate once a day to conduct business and hear what the abbot had to say. Beyond that were the abbot's quarters and a covered way, known as a slype, to allow access to the outside world, for Cistercian churches did not always have west doorways to allow the public in to participate in the sacrifice of the Mass. On the side opposite the church lay the kitchen and, beside it, the refectory, in front of which was usually water so that the monks could wash their hands before and after meals – the Cistercians being probably the first to introduce a sense of hygiene into Ireland. On the fourth side lay the stores and, above them on the first floor, a communal dormitory, from which steps led down to the western end of the church to facilitate the monks going down to say their night office.

With this orderly plan in mind, we can now approach the remains of Ireland's first great Cistercian monastery at Mellifont. Though it is ruined, we do not need the same amount of imagination as at Tara to work out what it looked like originally. Passing by a multi-storey tower which would have straddled the entrance to the monastery and acted as its necessary guardian centuries after it was founded, we come today to the car park, at the end of which is displayed a very useful plan to clarify the layout of the monastery that stretches out below.

You look down on the church at right-angles, as it were, standing as you are above the north transept, where there is an unusual arrangement of side-chapels – the ends changing from round to square and back to round, a system encountered nowhere else in the Cistercian building canon and one which would seem inherently impracticable in terms of roofing. It was probably the brainchild of the French Cistercians who came to supervise the building of the abbey in 1142, a Burgundian called Robert being the main architect in charge. After a while, Robert and the other French monks fell out with their Irish confrères and returned home. Nevertheless, building went on.

The church, not unusually long by Cistercian standards, had a short, square presbytery with a stone vault (long gone) over the high altar, and a nave separated from its side-aisles by an arcade. Its most unusual particular is the unexpected presence of a wooden-ceilinged crypt at the western end; this is likely to have had a structural rather than a liturgical function, and its purpose may be related to the location of the church beside the River Mattock, where the local king, Donnchad Ua Cerbaill, had granted the Cistercians a quiet place in the valley to build their monastery. The proximity of the western end of the church to the riverbank meant that stronger and deeper foundations were needed to support the west gable, particularly if the river were prone to flooding. The path of the river may also be responsible for the slightly skewed rectangle of the cloister garth, which is not exactly at a right-angle to the church.

Otherwise the Mellifont layout conforms to the normal Cistercian plan, the one unusual feature – Mellifont's finest – being the graceful octagonal lavabo (fig. 104) placed at the end away from the church and opposite the entrance to the monks' refectory. Built about 1200–1210, it has ground-floor arches cut from a warm and mellow, slightly yellowish sandstone. Its capitals are very sensitively carved with vegetal motifs and – in one instance – a bird, which has, alas, been badly damaged. The architectural detailing makes this one of the finest small gems of medieval building surviving anywhere in the country.

Originally it contained a central column from which vaults sprang and radiated fan-like to the surrounding walls. Frank Mitchell and Roger Stalley discovered parts of the stem of

Fig. 104: Despite its fragmentary condition, the beauty of the lavabo built at Mellifont around 1200 has been admired by succeeding generations, as seen in this watercolour now preserved in the Royal Irish Academy (Ms. 3.C.29, page 51).

157

the central column and these turned out – unusually for the Cistercians – to have been decorated with figure sculpture, though the subject-matter of the carvings has not yet been satisfactorily identified. (The fragments are now displayed in the attractive visitor centre beside the car park.)

This central column must also have acted as a fountain, the constant sound of flowing water bringing a soothing tranquillity to the cloister, and perhaps also conveying a symbolic message about the cleansing power of water in removing sin through the sacrament of baptism. Pipes which acted as the conduit for the water, siphoning it off at a higher level from the Mattock, were found by Liam de Paor in his excavations here in the 1950s.

At the same time, he discovered some of the double-capitals that formed part of the cloister itself – the only example in the late Romanesque style surviving in Ireland – and these have been built into a short reconstructed section adjoining the lavabo (see fig. 103, page 154). With its twin-shafts and scalloped capitals, partially with stylised foliate decoration, the design of this cloister was probably influenced from England (as was that of the lavabo).

Other than the lavabo, the main structure still standing at Mellifont is the chapter house (see fig. 102, page 153), seen on the left as you look down on the church from the car park. It was built around 1220 with an ornate doorway in the early English style and surmounted by an angel, as we know from an engraving that appeared in Wright's *Louthiana* (1748); the doorway was dismantled sometime within the following half century. It must have had a predecessor, built in the early stages of monastic construction and presumably before the church was consecrated with great pomp and circumstance in 1157, by which time Mellifont had already founded seven Irish daughter houses in various parts of the country.

The consecration had been preceded only five years earlier by one which was to be of more than just local significance. In 1152 a part of the proceedings of the Synod of Kells actually took place in Mellifont, and it was here that the final stamp of approval was given to the structure and location of Irish dioceses and archdioceses, a system that retains its effect down to the present day. In 1111 the Synod of Rathbreasail had, as we have seen, agreed that there were to be two archdioceses in Ireland – Armagh for the northern half and Cashel for the southern half. But by the late 1140s the reformed Irish clergy had expressed the desire to have the number increased to four, and, at a Synod that assembled in 1148 on St Patrick's Island, off the north Dublin coast at Skerries, St Malachy was deputed to go to Rome and ask that this request be fulfilled by the Holy See. St Malachy never made it to Rome, dying that same year in the arms of his great friend, St Bernard, at Clairvaux (his wish to stay with the Cistercians being finally fulfilled in death). But his demise did not prevent the message getting through, and four years later Mellifont experienced its greatest triumph – and the high-point of Cistercian influence in the country – when, amid the company of the bishops of Ireland and three thousand ecclesiastics, the papal legate, Cardinal Paparo, distributed the pallium (the official insignia of an archbishop's authority) to four archdioceses, Dublin and Tuam in addition to the two recognised earlier, Armagh and Cashel. The cardinal, probably the first of his rank ever to set foot in Ireland, 'appointed the archbishop of Armagh as primate over the other bishops' – the origin of the title 'Primate of All Ireland' which still attaches to the Archbishop of Armagh.

Twenty years later, this thriving monastery was said to have had a community of more than one hundred monks and three times that number of lay brothers. But, when the extant chapter house came to be built around 1220, it must have heard voices raised in discontent.

In 1216, the mother house at Clairvaux had been informed that 'enormities' existed at Mellifont and, with a view to reforming the community, had sent a delegation to its Irish daughter house to investigate. The abbot ordered his lay brothers to close the monastery's gates against the foreign visitors, but was deposed the following year.

Part of the problem was that the Irish Cistercian houses were split into two camps: there were those like Mellifont and its affiliated houses which were under the control of Irish abbots, and then there were others founded by the newly arrived Norman barons, who had put their own people in as abbots. The linguistic barrier made it difficult for the factions to talk and settle matters peacefully. Furthermore, the Irish opposed being taken over by those Normans who had come to be the secular rulers of much of the land around their monasteries, and were becoming less and less inclined to accept the dictates of the Cistercian order, based as it was in France – the country from which the barons had originally come. The man whom the great central monastery of Citeaux appointed to go to Ireland on a scrutinising visitation in 1228 was Stephen of Lexington, an Englishman, which again did not help matters.

The abbots of the monasteries affiliated to Mellifont were deposed, and Mellifont was given a new abbot, a man from Clairvaux. He resigned shortly afterwards when he discovered that some members of the community were planning to murder him. The Mellifont group of 'conspirators' was broken up and the abbeys they came from made subservient to Cistercian houses in England.

When Stephen finally managed to arrive at Mellifont, at the end of July 1228, he found that half of the monks had taken to the hills to avoid him, carrying most of the monastic valuables away with them. Some of the community were later allowed back (presumably with at least some of the valuables), but the escapees were ordered to go off to English and French houses of the order for penitential punishment.

The backbone of Irish resistance was defeated. English and French monks were installed to restore discipline, and the Anglo-Norman axis can be seen to have won out when Stephen ordered that no one should ever be allowed to enter an Irish Cistercian monastery who could not confess his sins in either French or Latin. Although King Edward II complained to the Cistercian mother house at Citeaux that only those who could swear they were not of English race were admitted to join the Mellifont community, by 1380 the monastery was again under Norman control when it was decreed that no 'mere Irishman' should be professed there. It was presumably Anglo-Norman money which had allowed the extension of the chancel of the Mellifont church in the mid-thirteenth century and the remodelling of the south transept around 1320, which saw the creation of the huge diamond-shaped piers with multiple shafts still visible at the crossing of nave and transepts, where – later again – a tower was erected that has long since collapsed.

Certainly Mellifont was among the richest of the Irish Cistercian abbeys during the later Middle Ages. By the time it came to be dissolved in 1539, it had only 21 monks, but it was still the second richest Cistercian house in Ireland, being in possession of about 5,000 acres in counties Louth and Meath, with a castle, five water-mills, many fisheries and boats – and ten rectories. By 1628 the Lordship of Mellifont increased the acreage ten times over.

Sir Edward Moore established a fortified house within the church in the 1560s. When his family finally abandoned it in 1727, it – and what remained of the church and cloistral buildings – became a quarry for building stone, leading to the ruins becoming the shadows of their former selves that we see today.

Fig. 105: This suitably romantic Boyne view of Trim, showing the massive block of the Norman castle on the right, appeared in Mr and Mrs S. C. Hall's Ireland *in the early 1840s.*

Trim Castle

The same Anglo-Normans who were involved in trying to get virtual control of some of the Irish Cistercian monasteries were also those who – at an earlier stage – had taken over the ownership of the rich lands adjoining the Boyne, for they were men with a keen eye for good soil. Within a few short years of their first arrival in Ireland, Henry II granted the Lordship of Meath in 1172 to Baron Hugh de Lacy, and the grant included most of the lands bordering the Boyne. We know that de Lacy immediately set about fortifying himself at Trim. His first building probably went up in flames when Rory O'Connor, King of Connacht, invaded the place in 1174, but de Lacy lost little time in replacing it with a new set of defences of a rather different kind (fig. 105). These included the large central stone tower that we see today, which would have been seen as a status symbol to cow the natives and impress fellow-Normans – including the king – as much as a defensive bastion. Kevin O'Brien of Dúchas has cleverly been able to extract original wood from holes in this tower, the tree-rings of which indicate that the ground floor had already been begun in 1174–5. The ground plan of de Lacy's castle has the shape of a Greek equal-armed cross – that is, a square tower from the centre of each side of which a smaller square tower protrudes. These subsidiary towers were provided with arrow loops to cover most – though not all – angles. The numerous angles involved made this central tower potentially liable to be undermined from the side by sophisticated siege machines. The castle was thus located on what was made into an island by diverting some of the water of the Boyne around the mound on which it was built, thereby giving an added defence.

There is no indication that the roughly D-shaped curtain wall enclosing the central tower was started at around the same time as the central tower. Nevertheless, to have left the tower standing on its own without any further protection would seem foolhardy, and so the curtain wall must have been at least planned not long after the tower was begun in the mid-1170s.

When Hugh de Lacy was murdered in 1186, the tower was apparently nowhere near completion, but an internal roof was placed over the two subdivided parts of the first floor in order to make the first two storeys useful and habitable, and one of the side-towers was provided with space to make a chapel.

Fig. 106: A barbican that once housed a drawbridge extends out from a tower of Trim Castle, and under the arch at its base flowed water in the moat which formerly made the whole castle into a fortified island.

Kevin O'Brien's wood samples do not show any evidence of further building activity in the central tower until about 1195, by which time Hugh de Lacy's son Walter had acceded to the Lordship, and Walter may well have been the man who largely succeeded in completing the central tower, possibly by 1200. The wood samples from this stage of construction indicate large squared timbers set deeply in the wall; these supported a hoarding just below roof level that served as a platform for archers and facilitated rapid circulation around the top of the castle – a defence vividly brought to life for film-goers when shown thus in *Braveheart* (1995), a movie partly shot on location in Trim.

When completed at the end of the twelfth century, Trim Castle was, according to Wolfgang Metternich, one of the most impressive castles in the Europe of its day, and it is one of Ireland's most significant monuments of the later Middle Ages.

As with its nearest Irish rival, Carrickfergus, on the shores of Belfast Lough, the lord would have lived in the castle, but the hall where entertainment took place, and where justice would have been meted out, lay on the inside of the curtain wall – in Trim's case, overlooking the Boyne in the northwestern corner of the enclosure. Its windows – almost certainly an Achilles' heel in the castle's defences – were blocked up sometime during the Middle Ages. Originally, the curtain wall would have enclosed the whole castle, but much of the side overlooking the Boyne collapsed and is no longer extant. However, as if to make up for it, the other two sides are still well endowed with towers, mostly rounded. The main tower, now giving entrance from the town via a ramp, has a vertical groove for a portcullis, and was once protected by a drawbridge over the diverted waters of the River Boyne. The same is true of the other interesting gate (fig. 106, page 161), the one at the southeastern corner, where the drawbridge lay between the town gate and a square tower – the barbican – outside it, forcing any attacker to go through a narrow passage and then be liable to attack from archers stationed on either side of the gate. It is in this town gate that Prince Hal (later King Henry V) and the 'Good Duke' Humphrey of Gloucester are thought to have stayed. Although Richard, Duke of York, is said to have held court here around 1450, the castle had largely been abandoned by this time.

Drogheda Town Walls

Another barbican, of a rather different kind, is found nearer the mouth of the Boyne, in the historic town of Drogheda, where the river's waters pass under a bridge for the last time before gliding gracefully into the Irish Sea. As the gateway to one of the richest areas of Ireland, Drogheda was destined to play an important role in the history of the Boyne. Who knows whether the fort of Millmount, which dominates the southern bank, may have been built on a Passage Grave like the one at Newgrange, meant to be seen from afar? Even at the dawn of the country's history, as we have seen, St Patrick landed somewhere near here before venturing up the river. The Vikings, too, would have rowed upriver, though they were prevented by Irish forces from making a more permanent landfall hereabouts. To judge by present traces, it was not really until the arrival of the Anglo-Normans in the twelfth century that Drogheda began to burgeon as a settlement of importance. Its very name, Droichead Átha, 'the bridge of the ford', suggests that its importance lay in being the lowermost ford where the river could be crossed on horseback.

Fig. 107: St Laurence's Gate stood outside the now-vanished east wall of Drogheda north of the Boyne in order to provide an added defence in controlling access to the town from land bordering the estuary of the river. It gets its name from a hospital that once stood nearby.

The Boyne was the dividing line in the later Middle Ages between the de Lacy Lordship of Meath to the south and the de Verdon lands in County Louth to the north. This circumstance, not to mention any rivalry, meant that two boroughs existed in Drogheda, one on each bank; although they were united politically in 1412, the division still remains in the existence of separate parishes within the town: St Mary's to the south and St Peter's to the north.

The division also meant that the town had two separate sets of town walls, one on the north and the other on the south. The area around the former St Mary's Church (Church of Ireland) still retains parts of the old south town walls.

The most significant remnant of the north wall is St Laurence's Gate (see page 89), which more than any other monument bears witness to the solidity and significance of this important medieval town (fig. 107, page 163). It is not, strictly speaking, a town gate but a barbican – a structure placed in front of the town gate as an outer protection, like the southeastern tower we have already seen at Trim Castle (see page 162). For a town that was – and still is – an important port, Drogheda needed to fortify itself against attack by land from the Irish or by sea from the Scots or anyone else. Consisting of two massive circular towers flanking a gateway, this was a fortification that was started in the thirteenth century but, as the later Middle Ages progressed, had to be raised in height to maintain its defensive capabilities – not once, but twice, as breaks in the masonry indicate. By no means Drogheda's tallest monument, it is nevertheless a forceful reminder of the town's commercial importance in the medieval period, and one of the most imposing pieces of urban architecture of its kind in the country. Its position as part of the old town defences is not always easy to appreciate because of the houses which have grown up around it in the last two hundred years, but it is clearly visible to anyone who knows where to look for it from the south side of the Boyne on the approach road from Dublin.

Newtown Trim

The town of Trim also had its town wall on the other side of the river from the castle, but the de Lacys knew how to spread themselves in ecclesiastical architecture as well. The Yellow Steeple has already been mentioned (see page 33), but more significant in the development of Trim, at least from our point of view, is a structure located about three kilometres downstream from the tower, and just upstream from where a lovely old-fashioned bridge crosses the Boyne at Newtown Trim (see fig. 18, page 39). Here we find a tall and gaunt-seeming building whose present state of conservation does not give an adequate idea of its former status and architectural grandeur. Its history is a re-run, in a slightly different way, of what we saw happening in the contrast between Monasterboice and Mellifont. Clonard, higher up the Boyne, was, as we have seen, an important monastery in the early centuries of Christianity in Ireland. St Malachy, the church reformer who was responsible for the Cistercian foundation at Mellifont in 1142, instituted a convent of Augustinian nuns at Clonard in 1144, and Hugh de Lacy, after he had taken over the Lordship of Meath, founded an Augustinian monastery for monks there too, sometime shortly before his death in 1186.

The convent was burned in 1171 by the infamous Diarmait MacMurrough, and in 1200 a small Irish army led by an O Ciardha from the area around the source of the Boyne plundered the monastery, which the Anglo-Normans had made the Cathedral of Meath, in place of the old Irish monastery which had provided bishops since the Synod of Rathbreasail in 1111. An Anglo-Norman Lord of Parliament, Simon de Rochfort, had himself made Bishop of Meath in 1192, occasionally even calling himself Bishop of Clonard. When the Irish burned Clonard in 1200 'to injure the foreigners that were in it', de Rochfort decided he had better bring his diocese under the closer military protection of Trim Castle. So in 1206 he moved the seat of his bishopric downstream from Clonard to Newtown Trim – which he called Novi-midia (New Meath).

To give his new location some legitimacy, he was able to call upon the old tradition that St Patrick had founded an Episcopal church at Trim. The seat of his bishopric was thenceforth to be the Augustinian Monastery of St Mary, which had been founded at the suggestion of St Malachy around 1140 and in due course, probably at the behest of Hugh de Lacy, had become a member of a Parisian branch of a religious order known as the Canons of St Victor. It is the remains of their monastery that loom large on the skyline at Newtown Trim today. It acted as the cathedral of de Rochfort's diocese of Meath, saving him the vast expense of having to build a separate cathedral of his own.

De Rochfort was not a man to think small and, in the same way that Trim Castle was to become one of the most impressive of its kind even beyond the bounds of Ireland, so also did Newtown Trim become one of the largest Anglo-Norman churches in the country, though thanks to a late-medieval truncation (seen in the plan, fig. 108, page 166) it would not necessarily give that impression today. He had grandiose ideas, and his building activity strongly suggests that he was out to impress. He was, indeed, rivalling Dublin, where Christ Church Cathedral was beginning to take its present form, and where the English King himself was ordering the building of his castle at the same time (1204) to act as his treasury.

The total length of the church originally was 56.7 m, a mere 2 m shorter than Christ Church; in the words of Christine Casey and Alistair Rowan, whose *North Leinster* volume in the *Buildings of Ireland* series offers the best treatment of the church, 'to walk down its length in the thirteenth century must have been an extraordinary experience'. They

Fig. 108: Plan of the Cathedral and Abbey of Newtown Trim (Christine Casey and Alistair Rowan, North Leinster).

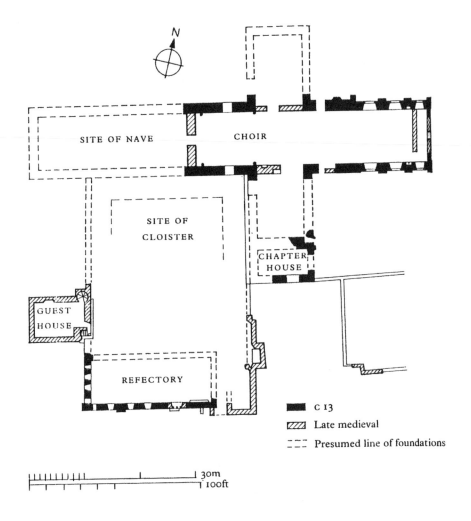

reproduce a reconstruction drawing of the choir, pointing out that it was roofed by one of the few large-scale Irish stone vaults outside Dublin (rivalry again!). The church was one long hall from east to west, with two large transepts leading off it. Where the nave once proudly stood is now a green field, and the tall north and south walls, still standing, are what remains of the original choir – the present east and west walls were a later addition. Sufficient survives of the choir to allow us to admire the rich mouldings and capitals that once adorned the windows, alternating with less ornate surrounds.

To the south and southwest of the church are still some remains of the old Victorine monastery, partially of the thirteenth century and partially of the fifteenth. To the former century belong fragments of the chapter house, adjoining which was the former south transept, and the refectory, looking out over the Boyne – which provides a splendid echo to anyone calling to it from a gate on the far side of the river. To the later medieval section of the ruins belongs the guest-house, which looks westwards towards Trim Castle. The Dillon tomb of 1586 in the adjoining parish church and the Priory of St John the Baptist are discussed elsewhere (see page 39 and fig. 109, page 168).

Medieval effigies

There is one effigy at Newtown Trim, and John Hunt suggested it might be that of Simon de Rochfort, the man responsible for building the grandiose church there, even if we can't be sure it was all finished by the time he died in 1224. It is one of the first of a series of medieval effigies for which County Meath is famous, and which ought to be ranked among the lesser-known gems of the Boyne Valley and surrounding areas. There is a similar, marginally earlier effigy of another ecclesiastic further downstream; formerly at Painestown, it is now built into the south wall of the Church of Ireland church in Slane (see page 65). It is unlikely to have been carved in the locality, however, and may have been brought to the banks of the Boyne from Dublin or even from England.

The Newtown Trim effigy, done in sandstone and now confined to a niche behind a locked grille, bears the traces of a crozier, suggesting that the figure depicted was a bishop; given that stylistic considerations would place it somewhere early in the thirteenth century, an identification with Simon de Rochfort seems quite reasonable. Unlike the man in life, the effigy has lost its head, which would have been carved as resting on a pillow and – like that from Painestown – was framed by foliate surrounds. Despite the weathering of centuries, the figure, which wears a chasuble, can be seen to have been of unusually high quality, which is just what we would have expected of the builder of the church in Newtown Trim.

Even if neither of these two effigies were produced in the Boyne Valley itself, the tradition of carving effigies survived the Black Death, which had a devastating effect on stone building and sculpture in Norman Ireland during and long after the years of its horrific devastation, 1348–50. This we can see from a knightly effigy at Kentstown, on the Nanny, which we cannot strictly say is part of the Boyne Valley but which we include here because it is such a rare and precious survival from this period. Housed in Kentstown's Church of Ireland church, it shows the area's former lord, Thomas de Tuite, Knight (who died apparently in 1363), wearing a jupon, with a mantle over his shoulders and his head resting on a tasselled pillar, his feet on a faithful dog.

The effigy of a bishop, now built into a wall in Slane Castle but possibly originally from Navan, has been ascribed to a period transitional between the fourteenth and fifteenth centuries; Elizabeth Hickey made the interesting suggestion that it may have been the covering for what is known as the Apostle Stone in a wooded part of the castle grounds.

By the fifteenth century, the descendants of the old Norman knights who had been granted land in the twelfth century had become, as the old saying went, 'more Irish than the Irish themselves'. With certain reservations, that went also for the great landowning families of County Meath – of whom the Plunketts and the Cusacks were the most prominent. They had been having effigies of themselves and their ladies carved for placing in the private family chapels they had built for themselves in the grounds of their great estates at places like Dunsany, Killeen and, north of the Boyne, at Rathmore. Time and vandals have not dealt a goodly hand to the effigies which survive at these locations, and it is not always easy to identify the person represented, even where inscriptions have been partially preserved. The knights are shown in their full armour, some probably inherited from ancestors and thus a bit antiquated, combining both chain mail and plates, and with a helmet or bascinet and (where preserved) a sword hanging at the waist. On the other side are their respective wives, wearing long voluminous gowns with tubular folds falling to the feet and extremely elaborate head-dresses that rise like two horns or turrets. Such were the lords and ladies of the Boyne Valley in the fifteenth century, living well off the profits of their vast estates but

Fig. 109: The double effigy of Sir Lucas Dillon and his wife, at Newtown Trim, dates from around 1586 and sits on a box-tomb bearing both their coats-of-arms. It is the finest piece of Elizabethan stone-carving in the Boyne Valley.

adding much to the sculptural and architectural heritage of their county. The tomb and effigy styles were imitated later by the Butlers and others in County Kilkenny in the sixteenth century.

But the sixteenth century has its own relevant effigies. One of these, at Dunfierth in County Kildare, represents a previous owner of Carbury Castle (see page 23) who died around 1548. Others bring us to later in the century, when a strong Elizabethan influence is detectable, with a whiff of Renaissance style. An example is the tomb of Sir Thomas Cusack and his family, formerly at Trevet but now preserved in fragments in the church on the Hill of Tara. Like other memorials of its kind in Ireland, it shows the knight kneeling on a prie-dieu facing his wife, with a number of their children flanking them on either side. The whole is accompanied by a long inscription in Latin (instead of English, as one would have expected), but this is now scarcely legible.

Finally there is the fine tomb (fig. 109) of Sir Lucas Dillon and his wife at Newtown Trim, mentioned above on pages 39 and 166. It shows the very high-relief effigies of Sir Lucas Dillon, Knight, and his wife Jane, daughter of James Bathe, of Athcarne, who had seven sons and five daughters. Sir Lucas was Chief Baron of the Exchequer and died around 1594. Though there is no inscription to tell us whose is the effigy, we can identify it as his through the Dillon and Bathe arms on the western end of the tomb-chest, where we have Sir Lucas and his wife portrayed kneeling on their prie-dieus, with the father having three of his sons behind him and the mother three of her daughters, the whole group placed beneath the engraved words 'DEUS/God'.

One of the other fine late-Elizabethan tomb-chests surviving in Ireland is also a Dillon tomb. It is preserved at Lusk in County Dublin.

Bective Abbey

Bective Abbey (fig. 110) is one of the most romantic-looking of all the monuments in the Boyne Valley. Situated in open countryside, it stands in the middle of a large field sloping gently down to the Boyne beside the bridge (fig. 111, page 170) which gave Mary Lavin the title of her first book of short stories (see page 44), and nestles beside a beech tree that turns a beautiful russet hue in the autumn. It is no surprise to find out that the monastery was given the name 'Beatitude of God' when founded for the Cistercians by Murchad O Melaghlin, King of Meath, in 1147. It was one of the daughter houses of Mellifont and, in various aspects, its story dovetails neatly with some of the late-twelfth- and early-thirteenth-century characters we have seen flitting across our path.

One of these was Hugh de Lacy, whom we have encountered as Lord of Meath and builder of Trim Castle. He was decapitated at Durrow in County Offaly in 1186, and his body was retained by the Irish who had carried out the murder. It was finally brought to Bective ten years later – although the head, ominously, was given to St Thomas's Abbey in Dublin, an Augustinian abbey of the Victorine congregation, to which Newtown Trim also belonged. St Thomas's, which had had many benefactions from de Lacy, was not content with the head alone: it wanted the whole body. A dispute thus arose between St Thomas's and Bective which went as far as Rome. The decision must have seemed a foregone conclusion when the man given the job of deciding the matter was none other than Simon de Rochfort, builder of the Meath monastery of Newtown Trim. He, however, ordered that the reunited head and body should be given a permanent resting place in St Thomas's in

Fig. 110: The thirteenth- to sixteenth-century ruins of Bective Abbey stand out in stark winter silhouette above the moving waters of the Boyne.

Fig. 111: Even in the eighteenth century, Bective Abbey was accompanied by a large tree, as seen in this engraving from Grose's Antiquities of Ireland – a view taken from the southern bank of the river.

Dublin. This can't have pleased the Cistercian congregation at Bective, who supported the Irish faction when it came to the confrontation between the Irish-ruled and Anglo-Norman-dominated Cistercian monasteries in the dispute that has come to be known as the Conspiracy of Mellifont (see page 159). At the very beginning of that row, the Abbot of Bective got involved on the Irish side in a riot in the order's monastery at Jerpoint, in County Kilkenny, when abbots of six Cistercian monasteries including Mellifont refused to allow access to visitors who had been sent to inspect the monastery by the general chapter of the order.

In the course of the dispute, the Abbot of Bective was accused of imprisoning a man in a tree-stump until he died, for which he was committed to St Bernard's old monastery of Clairvaux in France for trial. By 1227 he had been deposed, and the Prior of Beaubec in Normandy was appointed in his stead. By the time Stephen of Lexington came on his general visitation in 1228 (see page 159), Bective was in the hands of clerics whose sympathies were Anglo-Norman, not Irish. One of the few snippets that survive of the later religious history of Bective is that, in 1380, Richard II of England declared that no 'mere Irishman' or king's enemy should be admitted to the monastery. That did not prevent a subsequent monarch, in the rotund shape of Henry VIII, closing the monastery down in 1536, at which stage, according to an old tradition recorded in Lord Dunsany's *My Ireland* (1937), the students who left it to go to Trim took up half a mile of the road!

Its possessions at that stage included about 1600 acres of land, granges or out-farms, a water-mill and a fishing weir by the Boyne – despite a number of goods having been removed by the former abbot, John English, who had been pensioned off. Unvalued in all of this were the hall, roofed cloister and chambers, which were held to be necessary for the farmer who got the land at the Dissolution, one Thomas Agard, a civil servant who had come over to Ireland in the entourage of Thomas Cromwell . . . who, surprise surprise, had been Henry VIII's agent in dissolving the monasteries. Bective was Agard's reward for having become Vice-Treasurer of the Mint, and he took out a lease on the property in 1537. Not letting any Meath moss grow under his feet, he boasted that within three months he had already set up a cloth-weaving project at Bective – about which nothing was subsequently heard. He is the man who gave Bective the final form that we see today, a building complex that underwent many changes after its original foundation in 1147 as Mellifont's first daughter house.

In 1228, Bective was said to lie 'in a strongly fortified place', and in an anonymous eighteenth-century manuscript in the National Library (Ms. 912, page 92) it is described as having the oldest castle in Leinster,

> built by Maelseachlain, contemporary with Bryan Boroimhe [Boru]. It is reported that he sent for the purpose to Greece for architects and I am well informed by a gentleman that knows the parish very well that there is at present residing therein a family of the name of Greagach, that is, Greece.

The original twelfth-century monastery probably conformed to the usual Cistercian plan *à la* Mellifont: a church with aisled nave, choir and transepts, together with domestic and other buildings laid out around the cloister garth to the south. But little or nothing of

Fig. 112: The Architect *of 13 July 1878, published detailed plans and elevations of the Abbey of Bective, along with interior views of the cloisters.*

that original church remains. The south arcade of the nave is probably the earliest surviving part of the building, dating from sometime after 1274. Much of the present structure (fig. 112, page 171) dates from the fifteenth century when, as Lord Dunsany succinctly put it, 'the holy men for whom it was built had fear of grosser things than spiritual dangers, for though they prayed in their chapels they had battlements on their towers, and walls of great thickness!'

The numbers in the community must have dwindled as the western end of the church was abandoned, but the main impression given by this building phase is of a fortress (compare fig. 20, page 41). Two massive towers were built to provide protected living quarters for the abbot and doubtless also for some members of his remaining community. A third tower may have been built over the crossing of nave and transepts. Precisely who the presumed enemy was, history does not reveal, but at least a feeling of peace and calm must have

Fig. 113: A beautiful miniature representing Christ before either Caiaphas or Pilate on fol. 55v of Ms. 94 in the Library of Trinity College, Dublin, decorated a fourteenth-century English Book of Hours that would have been used for private devotional prayer in Bective Abbey during the later Middle Ages.

Fig. 114: A fifteenth-century cleric praying on a pedestal in a carving on a pier of the cloister in Bective Abbey was the subject of a Muriel Brandt watercolour dating from around the 1960s.

prevailed inside the walls among what Roger Stalley, the great expert on Irish Cistercian architecture, described as 'the most intimate and secluded of the Irish Cistercian cloisters'. One beautiful fourteenth-century English manuscript Book of Hours (fig. 113) that my have been used there for private reflection and devotion is now preserved as Ms. 94 in the Library of Trinity College, Dublin.

The cloister was also among the more decorative, for one of its piers bears a carving of an abbot on a footstool (fig. 114), holding a crozier and with a coat-of-arms emblazoned with fleurs-de-lis above his head. It is presumably a representation of the man who rebuilt the cloister, though who he was we do not know – so little is recorded of the monastery's fifteenth-century history. What may well be the carving of a bishop, taken from one of the two sides of the cloister that no longer survive, is built into the exterior of the wall of the church at Johnstown, near Kilcarn Bridge (see page 48).

To the threateningly defensive towers Agard added the fireplaces and mullioned windows to make the place more comfortable. His stay did not last long, in fact, for he sold the building and lands to one Andrew Wyse in 1552. Despite holding the important post of Vice-Treasurer for Ireland, Wyse got into financial difficulties, being eventually in such considerable debt to the Crown that he landed himself in prison in London for half a dozen years. Litigation with his wife and, after his death, between her and the queen was finally settled, and the property descended through the Fitton family and Robert Dillon (to whom there is a memorial in the church on the Hill of Tara) to the Boltons, who finally handed the abbey over to the State in 1894.

173

ATHLUMNY Castle ¼ M from Navan Co. of Meath.

Fig. 115: The watercolour of Athlumney Castle (with its seventeenth-century addition closest to us), painted by Gabriel Beranger during a visit to the Boyne Valley in 1775, is now preserved on page 7 of the Royal Irish Academy's album 3.C.30.

Athlumney Castle

There is a certain generic resemblance in the solidity of the towers at Bective and the oldest part of Athlumney Castle (fig. 115), which faces Navan across the Boyne. But, unlike Bective, Athlumney was a castle from the start, built in three stages that show the transition from the fortificatory style of the fifteenth century to the greater enlightenment, with larger windows, of the sixteenth/seventeenth century.

The oldest section is thus a tower-house, which formed part of a manorial settlement including a church, which still survives in ruins on the far side of the road. The Athlumney tower is rectangular in plan, with turrets jutting out from its four corners, one of which contains a wide spiral staircase. The tower is fairly well preserved right up to roof level, and even the gable is preserved on the north side. Sometime around 1600, a long house was added to the tower, the two touching only at one corner, where doors linked the two. The house, not much short of 30 m long, has three storeys, each with three windows, their mullions and transoms still surviving in the upper storeys, and with gables above each vertical set of windows. The mouldings above door and windows tend towards the Gothic rather than the Elizabethan in style; more typical of the end of the Virgin Queen's reign are the oriel window projecting out towards the road at the southern end and the tall chimneys rising from the otherwise uninteresting western flanks.

There is more story than history attached to Athlumney, but the Dowdall family is usually given as the builders. One of its noble scions, Sir Lancelot, is the subject of the most famous tale associated with the castle, which is best related in the words of Sir William Wilde in his *The Beauties of the Boyne and the Blackwater* (1849):

> Standing on the left bank of the Boyne, opposite this point, we cannot help recalling the story of the heroism of its last lord, Sir Launcelot Dowdall, who, hearing of the issue of the battle of the Boyne, and the fate of the monarch to whose religion and politics his family had been so long attached, and fearing the approach of the victorious English army, declared, on the news reaching him, that the Prince of Orange should never rest under his ancestral roof. The threat was carried into execution. Dowdall set fire to his castle at nightfall, and, crossing the Boyne, sat down on the opposite bank, whence, as tradition reports, he beheld the last timber in his noble mansion blazing and flickering in the calm summer's night, then crash amidst the smouldering ruins; and when its final eructation of smoke and flame was given forth, and the pale light of morning was stealing over that scene of desolation, with an aching and a despairing heart he turned from the once happy scene of his youth and manhood, and, flying to the Continent, shortly after his royal master, never returned to this country. All that remained of this castle and estate was forfeited in 1700.

It was probably at about this time that the last stage of the castle was built. In a footnote Sir William relates another, earlier, story of deceit and jealousy to explain the burning of the castle:

> It is said that two sisters occupied the ancient castles of Athlumney and Blackcastle, which latter was situated on the opposite bank of the river; and the heroine of the latter, jealous of her rival in Athlumney, took the following means of being revenged. She made her enter into an agreement, that to prevent their mansions falling into the hands of Cromwell and his soldiers, they should set fire to them at the same moment, as soon as the news of his approach reached them, and that a fire being lighted upon one was to be the signal for the conflagration of the other. In the mean time the wily mistress of Blackcastle had a quantity of dry brushwood placed on one of the towers of the castle, which, upon a certain night, she lighted; and the inhabitants of Athlumney perceiving the appointed signal, set fire to their mansion, and burned it to the ground. In the morning the deception was manifest. Athlumney was a mass of blackened, smoking ruins, while Blackcastle still reared its proud form above the woods, and still afforded shelter to its haughty mistress.

Wayside Crosses

During the fifteenth, sixteenth and seventeenth centuries, the people of Meath – and other counties as well, particularly Westmeath – had the pleasing custom of erecting stone crosses beside the road. The inscriptions on these usually ask a prayer for whomever erected them or for someone deceased. The crosses vary in size, type and decoration – and quality. County Meath alone has up to thirty-five such crosses covering a timespan of over two centuries, and these have all been documented in detail by Heather King, who has done Trojan work in making us aware of these little treasures, even if many are now in a fragmentary state.

Together they offer an attractive collection of sculpted figures, be it saints, Christ lying in the Virgin's lap (the *Pietà*) or the Crucifixion. These are presented on ringed or unringed crosses, with or without arms, and with or without inscriptions. This latter feature means that it is frequently very difficult to date the crosses. It is impossible here to do anything more than look at a small selection.

To inspect the oldest of our examples we will once more have to make an exception and go just outside the Boyne Valley, to Balrath, where close to the road on the opposite side to the Post Office there is a cross dating probably from the early sixteenth century. The face away from the road shows the figure of the crucified Christ, with his feet placed one on top of the other in the typical Gothic fashion, and with a very flowing perizonium (loincloth) tied in a prominent knot. Beneath are rather cruder decorations, including a cusped arch.

Equally appealing is the *Pietà* on the side facing the road, where the figure of Christ is placed awkwardly across the Virgin's lap like a small disintegrating doll. She is raising her left hand in sorrow to the pleated veil she wears around her head. The scene seems to have had a European inspiration. Beneath the group is a rather gauchely carved Latin inscription in raised lettering asking for a prayer for one Johannis Broin, whose name has not yet been identified among the pages of history.

The lower half of the shaft is occupied by a secondary inscription to the effect that Sir Andrew Aylmer of Mountaylmer, Bart., and his lady Catherine, had this cross beautified in 1727 'per H. Smith' – probably some relation of the great sculptor Edward Smyth, who created not only the Crucifixion in Navan (see page 51) but also many of the major carvings on the Custom House in Dublin, including the head of the River Boyne.

Also slightly outside the Boyne Valley, and belonging more correctly to the River Nanny, are two crosses in Duleek, both commissioned by Jennet Dowdall, who erected a number of crosses in or around 1600 to honour the memory of her husband, William Bathe of Athcarne, Justice of Her Majesty's Court of Common Pleas, who died in 1599. One, on the roadside at the entrance to Annesbrook House, has a long inscription on the west face giving details of the couple and asking a prayer for their respective souls; its other side gives us a variant of the Hail Mary. At the top of the cross are representations of the Crucifixion and the Virgin and Child.

Raised on a plinth at the western end of the village of Duleek is the second Jennet Dowdall cross (fig. 116), this time more fragmentary, but crowded with figure sculpture on the three sides not containing the inscription. Here we find Saints Peter, Patrick and Keenane (the local patron saint, Cianán) on the east face, Mary Magdalen and Saints James and Thomas on the north, and Saints Andrew, Catherine and Stephen on the south. Above a collar with Arms of the Passion there are some further figures which are, however, not easy to interpret.

Fig. 116: Standing on a stone platform at the western end of the village of Duleek is this stone cross raised in 1601 by Dame Jennet Dowdall to the memory of her first husband, William Bathe of Athcarne. It is decorated with niches enclosing figures of various saints including Peter, Patrick and Cianán (the local patron).

Fig. 117: The seventeenth-century White Cross at Athcarne bears a tenderly executed representation of the Virgin and Child which, despite its worn condition, betrays a probable foreign origin for the composition.

A further cross has been re-erected at Duleek, beside the road entering the village from the Drogheda side. It bears an attractive inscription with raised Gothic lettering, dated 1633, that asks for a prayer for Thomassina Berford.

Our final choice of wayside cross is the White Cross at Athcarne (fig. 117), which can be ascribed to the seventeenth century, though opinions differ as to where it should be placed within that century. The quality of the carving of the Mother and Child shines through, despite exposure to the elements for more than three hundred years, and the musculature of the highly unusual Christ figure, with Jansenistic raised arms, makes this the most sculptural of all the Meath crosses. Its sculptor clearly relied on a foreign model, possibly from somewhere in the Low Countries, in the same way that the Balrath *Pietà* was probably copied from a continental prototype.

The Battle of the Boyne

Other than the crosses, dealt with very selectively in the previous section, the seventeenth century – being troubled both politically and militarily – has left comparatively little behind in the Boyne Valley by way of visible monuments. It was the century which saw Cromwell break through the town wall of Drogheda and, in the name of a Holy War, slaughter thousands and banish others to slavery in the West Indies. But that was not the only disturbing conflict the valley has had to endure. There was another, a more famous one, which had European ramifications and which still casts its shadow over this island down to the present day: the Battle of the Boyne (fig. 118), which took place on 1 July (old style)/ 12 July (new style) in the year 1690.

The two main combatants were closely related by marriage: the Stuart King James II's daughter was married to William of Orange, and William was the son of James's sister. James had come to the throne of England in 1685, an event which gave Irish Catholics hope that more tolerant times were approaching and encouraged them to show symbols of their ancient faith by re-erecting crosses such as, only a few years later, the Market Cross in Kells. But the English Protestants found James's ascent of the throne disturbing, fearing he might curb them in the practice of their own religion.

James had the backing of Louis XIV of France, who was interested in furthering the Catholic cause in Europe. The Netherlandish William, Prince of Orange, was widely regarded as the leader of the Protestant cause on the continent, and saw his role not in an Irish context but as an effort to try to defeat the great French 'Sun King'. Despite blood being thicker than water, he was happy to see the English efforts to depose their new Stuart monarch, whose Catholic leanings they mistrusted, and was pleased to accept their offer of

Fig. 118: The dramatic depiction of the Battle of the Boyne painted in 1693 by the Dutch artist Jan Wyck (c.1640–1702), and now in the National Gallery of Ireland in Dublin.

179

the throne of England himself. Here were the makings of a war which was civil, political and religious – and a family fight to boot.

The deposed James took refuge in France, and William instructed his ageing general, the Duke of Schomberg, to subdue the Irish, whose leader, Richard Talbot, Earl of Tyrconnel and the Catholic Lord Deputy of Ireland, refused to submit to the new English monarch. Louis XIV encouraged James to take him on in Ireland and, in 1690, with 6,000 French troops, James landed in Kinsale and marched northwards to Dundalk, approaching his nephew and son-in-law William, who had landed with 35,000 troops in Carrickfergus on Belfast Lough. James, for his part, was joined by almost 20,000 Irish troops. The scene was set for a right royal confrontation.

William marched south, allegedly mounted on a white horse, and tradition has him riding on it down King William's Glen to assemble his forces at Oldbridge on the Boyne (fig. 119). James had already crossed the river to take up his position on the southern bank. William then sent a third of his forces across the River Mattock to cross the Boyne near Rossnaree (the Boyne was tidal up to Oldbridge). James dispatched his troops upstream on the south bank to deal with this flanking manoeuvre, and these two sections faced each other across boggy terrain all day without any further movement on either side. But William then succeeded in getting the main part of his army across the river at Oldbridge, where the bridge with white-painted lattice now spans the Boyne. There they were opposed, unsuccessfully, by the Jacobite troops. Having failed to dislodge William from his new position, the Irish infantry broke rank and fell back, covered by its cavalry, as William's own cavalry crossed the river en masse a little downstream at Drybridge. By then, however, the backbone of Jacobite resistance had been broken. James's forces retreated in good order to Duleek, later to go on and fight on another disastrous field, at Aughrim in County Galway.

Neither James nor his French forces would appear to have engaged in the battle themselves. The deposed king retreated hastily to Dublin where, according to legend, he commented to Tyrconnel's wife, 'Your countrymen, Madam, can run well' – to which she retorted, 'Not quite so well as your Majesty, for I see you have won the race.'

Giving no further support to his loyal Irish subjects, James retired forever to France, perhaps unaware – and certainly uncaring – about the sobriquet he had earned in the country which had been prepared to live and die for him: Seamus a'Chaca, 'James the Shit'.

William, too, left Ireland later in the year, to continue his own religious fight as the undisputed King of England, along with his consort, James's daughter Mary. The rest is history, forever regretted by the vanquished, for whom a dark century was inaugurated on that fateful day.

Bellinter House

By contrast, for those associated with the victors at the Battle of the Boyne, the following century would see them creating some of the finest architecture Ireland has ever seen, fitted with high-quality furniture, paintings, glass and silverware by the best of Irish artists and craftsmen.

There are many good eighteenth-century houses in the Boyne Valley, but, as almost all of them are presently privately owned, we will concentrate here on just one particularly fine example which, since being taken over by the Sisters of Sion in 1965, is open to the public as a retreat and conference centre. This is Bellinter House (fig. 120), the back of which overlooks a stretch of the Boyne between Bective and Navan while the front gives onto a lawn dominated by the amply spreading branches of a wonderful weeping beech tree.

The house was built by John Preston, brewer and Member of Parliament, whose son, Lord Tara, built the bridge just downstream across the Boyne in 1813. The house was designed by Richard Castle or Cassels, an architect of German origin, around 1750, but how far building had proceeded before Castle's death the following year is not known. It is a very good example of a typical Irish country house of the period, done in Palladian style: it has a central two-storey block with flanking pavilions, also of two storeys but lower in height, from which walls curve out at the end to provide access to yards and gardens through gateways decorated with rococo urns. The single-storey section which helps to string out the façade, and to emphasise the difference in height between the main block and

Fig. 120: The fine Palladian mansion built at Bellinter from 1750 onwards by John Preston, MP, after designs by Richard Castle (or Cassells) who died while it was in the process of construction. It is now a successful retreat house and conference centre run by the Sisters of Sion.

Fig. 121: The stucco panels of c. 1750 in the hall of Bellinter House display military trophies such as this one, with weapons, flags and a lion's head.

the pavilions that flank it, shows the only major changes to the frontage since the house was built, as Gothic windows were inserted in the nineteenth century. Each storey of the central block has six windows, the two central ones on the ground floor holding the main door tightly between them, all three elements being united by a pediment above. On the first floor, the niche intended originally for a statue seems to be jammed in even more tightly between the centre windows than the door in the floor below.

Steps lead up to the entrance, through which you come directly into a hall with a large chimneypiece, fine plasterwork, including a strong Doric cornice, and military trophies (fig. 121). Two niches flank the door to the salon, straight ahead, which is delicately ornamented in rococo stuccowork in the manner of Robert West. Off it open two further rooms that overlook the Boyne at the back of the house.

One of the most remarkable features of the house is the splendid, if narrow, spiral staircase to the right of the hall. Because this was for the servants, it goes all the way from top to bottom of the house. The more grandiose family staircase leads off to the left, rising to the first-floor lobby, the centre of which is lit by an attractive oval lantern whose light airiness is diminished by the heavy decorated stucco beams that pretend to play a role in its support.

It is good to see the Sisters of Sion keeping as much as possible of Bellinter House in its original condition while at the same time changing its use from private home to conference and retreat centre.

Fig. 122: The chancel of St Peter's Church of Ireland church in Drogheda is decorated with wonderful late-baroque stuccowork of c. 1752, which surrounds a later monument to Francis Leigh. The memorial on the left commemorates Henry Singleton, recorder of Drogheda and later Lord Chief Justice of Ireland.

St Peter's Church of Ireland Church, Drogheda

At almost exactly the same time that Richard Castle was starting work on Bellinter, the Drogheda architect Hugh Darley was busying himself with the construction of a very different building, although also in the Palladian style: St Peter's Church (Church of Ireland), whose graceful tower and spire dominate Drogheda's town centre. The church stands on the site of an earlier and probably very much larger medieval church, some dressed stones of which are preserved. Darley was commissioned to demolish the older building in 1748 to make way for his new one, which was already well advanced when Swift's friend Mary Delany visited it in 1752.

The doorway, with a rounded fanlight illuminating the porch within, stands at the base of a massive central square tower that recedes upward in diminishing stages until topped by a balustrade, above which is the much slenderer spire, designed around 1780 by Francis Johnston to replace the original pyramidal stone steeple. The north and south walls each have two storeys of early Gothicising windows, a feature whose purpose becomes clear when you enter the splendidly elegant, warming interior and see that there is a gallery that runs all the way around the nave, being supported by pillars which continue up to the ceiling – an idea Darley may have got from some Dublin churches built earlier in the century, though originally conceived by Sir Christopher Wren in London.

In this imposing interior, all eyes look first to the chancel, where the highpoint is plasterwork done by an unidentified stuccodore, with lively birds dominating the vertically ornamented panels that flank the east window. More remarkable, however, is the decoration of the north wall (fig. 122) where a wonderful late-Baroque shield-like frame contains a diversity of elements – including fruit and flowers and cornucopias – and which branches out on top into angular garlands. Just around the corner from it is the pulpit, which has a fine Stapleton monument of *c.* 1780 above it. Some of the stucco was sadly and badly damaged by an irrational arson attack in 1999, but the whole interior has now been so superbly restored that no trace of the fire remains and the church has reverted to being what Casey and Rowan describe in their *North Leinster* volume as among 'the best provincial churches erected in Ireland during the eighteenth century and also one of the most richly endowed, patronised by, among others, the Marquis of Drogheda and the Archbishop of Armagh'.

Inside the door of the church is a medieval stone font dating to about 1500, with the Twelve Apostles and a Baptism of Christ, while outside, in the grounds, is the chilling cadaver effigy of Sir Edmund Goldyng (discussed more fully on page 89).

In the nineteenth century the Catholics built in West Street their own fine Church of St Peter, which the architectural historian of Drogheda, William Garner, described as one 'of the finest Gothic Revival churches in the country'. But the town's, and also the Boyne Valley's, finest nineteenth-century architectural achievement is undoubtedly the great viaduct erected over the Boyne, which has already been discussed in some detail elsewhere (see page 91).

This volume is not intended to cover the twentieth century in this honeyed valley. As a brief word of conclusion, however, we can say that it was in that century – following the great pioneering work of Sir William Wilde in the Victorian era – that the general public's appreciation of the importance, national and international, of the ancient monuments of the Boyne Valley really blossomed. It is to be hoped that this book will help further stimulate the public interest in the valley's treasures.

Selected Works Consulted

Barrow, Lennox. *The Round Towers of Ireland*. Dublin 1979.

Bhreathnach, Edel. *Tara. A select bibliography*. Dublin 1995.

Bhreathnach, Edel. 'Cultural identity and Tara from Lebor Gabála Érenn to George Petrie'. In *Discovery Programme Reports: 4*, Dublin 1996, 85–98.

Bhreathnach, Edel and Conor Newman. *Tara*. Dublin 1995.

Black, Eileen. *Drawings, paintings and sculptures. The Catalogue. MAGNI (Museums and Galleries of Northern Ireland)*. Belfast 2000.

Boylan, Henry. *The Boyne. A Valley of Kings*. Dublin 1988.

Bradley, John. 'The topography and layout of medieval Drogheda', *County Louth Archaeological and Historical Journal* 19 (2), 1978, 98–127.

Bradley, John. 'St. Patrick's Church, Duleek', *Ríocht na Midhe* 7(1), 1980–81, 40–51.

Bradley, John. 'The medieval towns of Meath', *Ríocht na Midhe* 8, 1988–89, 30–49.

Bradley, Richard. 'Stone circles and Passage Graves – a contested relationship'. In Gibson, Alex and Derek Simpson (eds.), *Prehistoric ritual and religion. Essays in honour of Aubrey Burl*, Stroud 1998, 2–13.

Brady, John. 'Anglo-Norman Meath', *Ríocht na Midhe* 2, 1961, 38–45.

Buckley, Victor M. and P. David Sweetman. *Archaeological Survey of County Louth*. Dublin 1991.

Byrne, Francis John. *Irish Kings and High Kings*. London 1973. Reprinted 2002.

Carew, Mairéad. *Tara and the Ark of the Covenant*. Dublin 2003.

Casey, Christine and Alistair Rowan. *North Leinster*. The Buildings of Ireland. London 1993.

Cogan, Rev. A. *The Diocese of Meath, ancient and modern*. Dublin 1862–70.

Condit, Tom (ed.). *Brú na Bóinne – Newgrange, Knowth, Dowth and the river Boyne*. Supplement to Archaeology Ireland, Vol. 11, No. 3, Bray 1997.

Condit, Tom and Gabriel Cooney. *Newgrange, Co. Meath: Neolithic religion and the mid-winter sunrise*. Archaeology Ireland Heritage Guide No. 8, Bray 1999.

Condit, Tom and Derek Simpson. 'Irish hengiform enclosures and related monuments'. In Gibson, Alex and Derek Simpson (eds.), *Prehistoric Ritual and Religion. Essays in honour of Aubrey Burl*, Stroud 1998, 45–61.

Corcoran, Moira. 'The Boyle O'Reilly stone (a sequel)', *Ríocht na Midhe* 5(3), 1973, 95–96.

Cromwell, Thomas. *Excursions through Ireland*. Vol. II, London 1820.

Delany, Ruth. *Ireland's Royal Canal*. Dublin 1992.

De Paor, Liam. 'Excavations at Mellifont Abbey, Co. Louth'. *Proceedings of the Royal Irish Academy* 68 C, 1969, 109–64.

De Paor, Liam. *St. Patrick's World*. Dublin 1993.

Dillon, Myles. *The Cycles of the Kings*. London/New York 1946.

Discovery Programme Reports: 2. Project results 1993. Dublin 1995.

Dronfeld, Jeremy. 'Subjective vision on the source of Irish megalithic art', *Antiquity* 69, 1995, 539–49.

Ellison, Canon C. 'Some aspects of Navan history', *Ríocht na Midhe* 3(1), 1963, 33–56.

Ellison, Canon Cyril. *The Waters of the Boyne and Blackwater: A Scenic and Industrial Miscellany*. Dublin 1983.

Eogan, George. *Knowth and the Passage-tombs of Ireland*. London 1986.

Eogan, George. 'Prehistoric and early historic culture change in Brugh na Bóinne'. *Proceedings of the Royal Irish Academy* 91 C, 1991, 105–32.

Eogan, George. 'Knowth before Knowth', *Antiquity* 72, 1998, 162–72.

Eogan, George and Helen Roche. 'A Grooved Ware wooden structure at Knowth, Boyne Valley, Ireland', *Antiquity* 68, 1994, 322–30.

Eogan, George and Helen Roche. *Excavations at Knowth 2*. Dublin 1997.

Fairtlough, Harry and Jackie Rooney. 'In Our Museum: The Banner Room', *Journal of the Old Drogheda Society* 3, 1978–79, 19–26.

Fenwick, Joe. 'A panoramic view from the Hill of Tara, Co. Meath', *Ríocht na Midhe* 9(3), 1997, 1–11.

FitzGerald, Lord Walter. 'Stackallan Churchyard', *Journal of the Association for the Preservation of the Memorials of the Dead. Ireland* 8, 1912, 612–14.

FitzGerald, Lord Walter. 'Two Colley inscriptions in the Castle Carbury churchyard; with notes on the founder of the family', *Journal of the County Kildare Archaeological Society* 8, 1915–17, 369–87.

Galway, Fiona. 'Meath tower houses', *Ríocht na Midhe* 7(4), 1985–86, 28–59.

Garner, William. *Drogheda. Architectural heritage*. Dublin 1986.

Graves, Robert Perceval. *Life of Sir William Rowan Hamilton*. Vol. I, London 1882.

Gwynn, Aubrey. *The Irish Church in the 11th and 12th centuries* (ed. Gerard O'Brien). Dublin 1992.

Gwynn, Aubrey and R. Neville Hadcock. *Medieval religious houses Ireland*. London 1970. Reprinted 1988.

Harbison, Peter. *Irish High Crosses with the figure sculptures explained*. Drogheda 1994.

Harbison, Peter. *Cooper's Ireland. Drawings and notes from an eighteenth-century Gentleman*. Dublin 2000.

Healy, Elizabeth. *A Literary Tour of Ireland*. Dublin 1995.

Hickey, Elizabeth. *I send my love along the Boyne*. With illustrations by Nano Reid. Dublin 1966. Reprinted 2003.

Hickey, Elizabeth. *Clonard. The story of an early Irish monastery 520–1202*. Leixlip 1998.

Hobson, R.B. 'David Jebb of Slane', *Ríocht na Midhe* 8(3), 1990/91, 36–40.

Hunt, John. *Irish Medieval Figure Sculpture, 1200–1600*. Dublin/London 1974.

Kerrigan, Paul M. *Castles and fortifications in Ireland, 1485–1945*. Cork 1995.

Killanin, Lord and Michael Duignan. *The Shell Guide to Ireland*, 2nd ed. London 1967.

King, Heather. 'Late medieval crosses in County Meath, *c.* 1470–1635', *Proceedings of the Royal Irish Academy* 84 C, 1984, 79–115.

King, Heather. 'Irish wayside and churchyard crosses, 1600–1700', *Post-Medieval Archaelogy* 19, 1985, 13–33.

Leask, H.G. *Irish Castles and Castellated Houses*. Dundalk 1941.

Ledwidge, Francis. *The Complete Poems*. Newbridge 1997.

Lenehan, Patrick. 'Edward Smyth. Dublin's sculptor', *The GPA Irish Arts Review Yearbook 1989/90*, 67–76.

Longford, Lady Elizabeth. 'Wellington and the Irish connection', *Ríocht na Midhe* 9(1), 1994/1995, 51–60.

Lyons, Mary. *Illustrated Incumbered Estates Ireland, 1850–1905*. Whitegate 1993.

McGowan, Kenneth. *The wonders of the Boyne Valley*. Dublin, no date.

McKillop, James. *Fionn mac Cumhaill, Celtic myth in English literature*. Syracuse, N.Y. 1986.

McNeill, Tom. *Castles in Ireland. Feudal power in the Gaelic world.* London/New York 1997.

Matthews, Seamus. 'John Boyle O'Reilly – The early years', *Journal of the Old Drogheda Society* 11, 1998, 45–57.

Metternich, Wolfgang. *Burgen in Irland. Herrschaftsarchitektur im Hochmittelalter*. Darmstadt 1999.

Mitchell, G.F. 'The evolution of Townley Hall', *Irish Georgian Society Bulletin* 30, 1987, 3–61.

Mitchell, Frank and Michael Ryan. *Reading the Irish Landscape*. Dublin 1997.

Moore, Michael J. *Archaeological Inventory of County Meath*. Dublin 1987.

Moroney, Anne-Marie. 'Winter sunsets at Dowth', *Archaeology Ireland* 13(4), 1999, 29–31.

Newman, Conor. *Tara. An archaeological survey*. Discovery Programme Monographs 2. Dublin 1997.

O'Brien, Jacqueline and Peter Harbison. *Ancient Ireland from Prehistory to the Middle Ages*. London 1996.

Ó Cairbre, Fiacre. 'William Rowan Hamilton (1805–1865); Ireland's greatest mathematician', *Ríocht na Midhe* 11, 2000, 124–50.

O'Dwyer, Barry. *The conspiracy of Mellifont, 1216–1231*. Medieval Irish History series, 2. Dublin 1970.

Ó hÓgáin, Dáithí. *Myth, Legend & Romance: An encyclopaedia of the Irish folk tradition*. London 1990.

O'Keeffe, Peter and Tom Simington. *Irish Stone Bridges; History and Heritage*. Blackrock 1991.

O'Kelly, Claire. *Guide to Newgrange*. Wexford 1967.

O'Kelly, Michael J. *Newgrange. Archaeology, art and legend*. London 1982.

O'Kelly, Claire and M.J. 'The tumulus of Dowth, County Meath', *Proceedings of the Royal Irish Academy* 83 C, 1983, 135–90.

O'Meara, Liam. *A lantern on the wave: A study of the life of the poet Francis Ledwidge*. Dublin 1999.

Ó Ríordáin, Séan P. *Tara. The monuments on the Hill*. Dundalk, 3rd ed., 1960.

O'Sullivan, William. 'Medieval Meath manuscripts', *Ríocht na Midhe* 7(4), 1985–86, 3–21.

Ray, T.P. 'The winter solstice phenomenon at Newgrange, Ireland: accident or design?', *Nature 337*, 26 January 1989, 343–45.

Reeves-Smyth, Terence. *Irish castles*. Belfast 1995.

Reynolds, James. 'Jonathan Swift – Vicar of Laracor', *Ríocht na Midhe* 4(1), 1967, 41–54.

Roche, Helen. 'Late Iron Age activity at Tara, Co. Meath', *Ríocht na Midhe* 10, 1999, 18–30.

Roe, Helen M. 'Cadaver effigial monuments in Ireland', *Journal of the Royal Society of Antiquaries of Ireland* 99, 1969, 1–19.

Roe, Helen M. *Medieval Fonts of Meath*. No place, 1988.

Roe, Helen M. *Monasterboice and its monuments*. No place, 1993.

Ryan, John. *Irish Monasticism. Origins and early development.* Dublin/Cork 1931.

Salter, Mike. *Castles and stronghouses of Ireland.* Malvern 1993.

Slavin, Michael. *Tara*. Dublin 1996.

Stalley, Roger. *Cistercian monasteries of Ireland.* London/New Haven 1987.

Stalley, Roger. 'The Anglo-Norman keep at Trim; its archaeological implications', *Archaeology Ireland* 6(4), 1992, 16–19.

Stalley, Roger. 'Decorating the lavabo; Late Romanesque sculpture from Mellifont Abbey'. *Proceedings of the Royal Irish Academy* 96 C, 1996, 237–64.

Stokes, Whitley. *The Tripartite Life of St. Patrick*. 2 vols. London 1887.

Stout, Geraldine. 'Embanked enclosures of the Boyne region', *Proceedings of the Royal Irish Academy* 91 C, 1991, 245–84.

Stout, Geraldine. *The Bend of the Boyne. An archaeological landscape.* The Irish Treasure series. Dublin 1997.

Stout, Geraldine. 'The bend of the Boyne, County Meath'. In F. H. A. Aalen, Kevin Whelan and Matthew Stout (eds.), *Atlas of the Irish Rural Landscape*, Cork 1997, 299–315.

Stout, Geraldine. *Newgrange and the Bend of the Boyne*. Cork 2002.

Sweeney, Tony. *Irish Stuart Silver*. Blackrock 1995.

Sweetman, P. David. 'Archaeological excavations at Trim Castle, Co. Meath, 1971–74', *Proceedings of the Royal Irish Academy* 78 C, 1978, 127–98.

Sweetman, P. David. 'An earthen enclosure at Monknewtown, Slane, Co. Meath', *Proceedings of the Royal Irish Academy* 76 C, 1976, 25–72.

Sweetman, P. David. 'A late Neolithic/Early Bronze Age pit-circle at Newgrange, Co. Meath', *Proceedings of the Royal Irish Academy* 85 C, 1985, 195–221.

Sweetman, P. David. 'Archaeological excavations at St. John's Priory, Newtown, Trim, Co. Meath', *Ríocht na Midhe* 8(3), 1990–91, 88–104.

Sweetman, David. *The medieval castles of Ireland*. Cork 2000.

The Murray Collection. Catalogue of the collection of Irish Antiquities formed by the late Thomas R. Murray of Edenderry, Kings County. University of Cambridge Museum of Archaeology and Ethnology. Cambridge 1901.

Thomas, Avril. *The walled towns of Ireland*. 2 vols. Blackrock 1992.

Todd, James H. *The Irish version of the Historia Britonum of Nennius*. Dublin 1848.

Trench, C.E.F. 'William Burton Conyngham (1733–1796)', *Journal of the Royal Society of Antiquaries of Ireland* 115, 1985, 40–63.

Trench, C.E.F. *Slane. Slane town trail. Newgrange*. Slane, 2nd ed., 1987.

Wilde, William R. *The Beauties of the Boyne, and its Tributary, the Blackwater*. Dublin 1849. Reprinted Headford 2003.

Willmot, G.F. 'Three burial sites at Carbury, Co. Kildare', *Journal of the Royal Society of Antiquaries of Ireland* 58. 1938, 130–42.

Index

Italicised numbers indicate pages of illustrations.

Picture Acknowledgements

The photographs in this book have been reproduced by kind permission of the following. The publishers have made every effort to trace the copyright holders and apologise in advance for any unintentional omissions. We will be pleased to insert the appropriate acknowledgement in any subsequent edition of this publication.

Half title, fig. 12: Photo: Brenda Fitzsimons. By courtesy of *The Irish Times*

Title page, pp 8–9, figs 2, 4–6, 8, 10–11, 13–14, 17, 19–21, 24–7, 29, 31, *33–4*, 36–7, 40, 43, 45–6, 48–50, 53, 56–8, 64–5, 67, 73–4, 78, 88–90, 92, 98–101, 103, 106–7, 110, 116–17: © Tom Kelly

Fig. 1: After William Wilde's *The Beauties of the Boyne*

Figs 3, 7: Reproduced by permission of University College Dublin Library

Figs 9, 28, 51, 70, 79, 86: By courtesy of the National Museum of Ireland

Figs 15, 23: By courtesy of the National Portrait Gallery, London

Figs 16, 104: By permission of the Royal Irish Academy © RIA

Figs 18, 32, 55, 62, 91: Courtesy of the National Library of Ireland

Fig. 22: Reproduced by kind permission of the artist, Pat Phelan

Fig. 30: Courtesy of Corbis

Figs 35, 72, 83–4, 115: Courtesy of the Royal Irish Academy © RIA. Photo: Brian Lynch

Fig. 38: Photo: Brendan Dempsey. Private Collection

Fig. 39: By courtesy of James Adam Salerooms

Fig. 41: Private Collection, Courtesy of Pyms Gallery, London

Figs 42, 118: By courtesy of the National Gallery of Ireland

Figs 44, 61, 97: From Cromwell's *Excursions*. Courtesy of the Neptune Gallery Dublin.

Fig. 47: Courtesy of Hulton Getty

Figs 52, 93, 94, 96: Peter Harbison

Fig. 54: Hugh Doran

Fig. 59: Reproduced by kind permission of An Post ©

Fig. 60: From *The Dublin Penny Journal*

Fig. 63: Photo: Brendan Dempsey. Private collection

Fig. 66: Photo: David Davison/The Irish Picture Library

Fig. 68: By courtesy of Jan de Fouw

Figs 69, 113: Courtesy of the Board of Trinity College Dublin

Figs 71, 75: Courtesy of Dúchas The Heritage Service. Photo: Con Brogan

Figs 76–7, 80–82, 85, 87, 109: Courtesy of Dúchas The Heritage Service

Fig. 95: © Bord Fáilte Photographic. Photo: Brian Lynch

Figs 102, 111: From Grose's *Antiquities of Ireland*. By courtesy of the Neptune Gallery, Dublin

Fig. 105: From Hall's *Ireland*. By courtesy of the Neptune Gallery, Dublin.

Fig. 108: Yale University Press (Pevsner Architectural Guides, The Buildings of Ireland series).

Fig. 112: From *The Architect*. By courtesy of the Neptune Gallery, Dublin

Fig. 114: Watercolour by Muriel Brandt. Reproduced by courtesy of the author

Fig. 119: Photograph reproduced with the kind permission of the Trustees of the National Museums & Galleries of Northern Ireland. Photograph © Ulster Museum

Fig. 120: Irish Architectural Archive (Lord Rossmore)

Fig. 121: Irish Architectural Archive (David Davison)

Fig. 122: Photo: David Davison/The Irish Picture Library